TEN STEPS TO
THE GOOD LIFE

TEN STEPS TO
THE GOOD LIFE

J. John

HODDER AND STOUGHTON
LONDON SYDNEY AUCKLAND TORONTO

Dedicated to
Eric Delve,
pastor, teacher, evangelist
and friend

British Library Cataloguing in Publication Data

John, J.
  Ten steps to the good life.
  1. Ten Commandments – Critical studies
  I. Title
  241.52

  ISBN 0-340-51747-6

PREFACE

Many people help one to write a book and I have many people to thank for their support and guidance. This includes all those who pray for my work and our prayer group, especially acknowledging the faithfulness of Kenneth and Mary Habershon, David and Joyce Huggett, Peggy Wright, Len and Dorinda Miller, and Roger and Ginny Campbell. I am grateful to all my Trustees and Dave and Janie Beales for their support and wisdom and also my spiritual adviser, Father Thomas. Thanks to Hodder & Stoughton my publishers and my inspiring editor Carolyn Armitage.

I owe a good deal to discussions with various people, those memorable being with Phil and John (for down-to-earth conversations especially after a curry!); to Sharon Whorlow for constantly reminding me of practical theology and simplicity, to Lisa Opie for her friendship and much encouragement, and to Shirley Brown for all her support. Many thanks to Lois Thompson who continues to provide a well of material, and to my assistant Dave Edwards for the many hours spent in research. More than one thank you to my secretary Jackie Maugham for managing to decipher my notes and type the manuscript. Special, special thanks to Mary Juckes and Ric Thorpe – two wonderful people. Thank you Mary and Ric for editing the book. Your honest reactions and corrections helped me to think and re-think and to re-write. It occurs to me to add that wherever I have borrowed I have tried to give due credit. However, for any material that I may have unconsciously remembered and innocently re-written, I ask absolution! I've got a vague feeling that my friend Roger Simpson gave me a few things – I haven't a clue what or when or where.

Thanks especially to my wife Killy for her wisdom in all our discussions and my two sons Michael and Simeon with whom I have found life to be a great happening, a life full of surprises.

Finally, my thanks go most of all to the Christ for whom all this has been attempted.

J. John
Nottingham 1990

INTRODUCTION

When you think of all the libraries of law books, it is amazing how wide a span this simple rainbow of the ten commandments arches. Family rights, property rights, the rights of God and the rights of the individual are all included. Someone once said that man is an able creature, but he has made 32,647,389 laws and has not yet improved on the ten commandments. The ten commandments are the best laws ever made – and the basis for our legal system today.

Now and then, however, someone who has been educated beyond his intelligence believes that the music needs a new arrangement. He dismisses the ten commandments as being no longer fashionable. He insists that a new world needs a new ethic. He basically wants to know why modern men should be burdened with the primitive code of a nomadic tribe which lived under skin tents in an ancient desert!

The tents, the tribe and the desert are ancient – this is not in dispute. But if you change the tents to flats and houses, if you change the nomadic tribe to travelling executives in business suits with briefcases, if you change the desert to a city, it remains true that human nature is still what it always was. Of course things have changed. The clicking abacus has become the sophisticated computer. The creaking ox-cart has become the super-jet. But fire is still fire, water is still water and mankind is still mankind. We still have the same pitfalls as ever.

That is why, long before God gave Moses the ten

commandments written on tablets of stone, He had engraved them on the fleshy tablet of the human heart. They were inside us, almost like instincts. Who was not aware in his heart that he should worship His Maker? Who ever doubted that it was wrong to lie or steal or murder or commit adultery?

There is a true story about a Christian prison governor, preaching in the prison chapel, who took as his theme the ten commandments. Some of the prisoners came up to him and said, "That's no good, sir, you can't live the ten commandments in the twentieth century." So the Governor put a notice up all over the prison, "No longer will the ten commandments be obeyed in this prison." The first day a man came up and said, "Someone has stolen my pen." On the second day a man came up and said, "Someone has stolen my cigarettes." At the end of the week, the Governor said to a young man, "I want to invite you to a special tea. Don't have any supper the previous night. It's going to be a fantastic meal, so have no breakfast, no lunch. Come at 5.00 p.m." The young man came at 5.00 p.m. and all that was left was a few crumbs because the Governor started the tea at 4.00 p.m. The young man was furious and said, "You can't live like this. You're the Governor of this prison. You said come at 5.00 p.m. and I believed you", but the Governor said, "Yes, but we are not living by the ten commandments in this prison." By the end of a fortnight, by popular demand by over two-thirds of the prison, the ten commandments were brought back to regulate the life in that prison.

Law is at the heart of liberty. Laws do not restrict us – they free us to live in order and harmony. St Augustine phrased the Christian law as "Love God and do what you like." In other words, love God and therefore His instructions. Many people have gone for a different motto, "Do what you like" and, soon after, rush to a psychoanalyst to find out "why I no longer seem to like anything".

The ten commandments are only like the embossed numerals on the dial of everyman's conscience. They are not made for any particular period in history. They were based on human nature and therefore were commandments for all seasons, for all centuries, as universal and perpetual as honour and truth.

Commandments one to four deal with our behaviour towards God. Commandments five to nine deal with our behaviour towards mankind. The tenth commandment deals with our thoughts. The commandments are concerned with what we think, not just what we do. Wrong ideas precede wrong actions.

The aim of this book is to guide Christians as to what our attitude and behaviour should be to God and other people. We can so easily call ourselves Christians because we believe and trust in Jesus Christ and not do anything else, but belief needs to be validated in action. The ten commandments are God's irreducible minimum for living, ten steps to the good life. We therefore need to know them and by God's grace and strength endeavour to live them.

1

> I am the Lord your God, who brought you out
> of Egypt, out of the land of slavery.
> You shall have no other gods before me.
> (Exodus 20:2–3)

The first commandment begins with our relationship with God. The commandment is a positive statement that God makes about who He is. He is not an abstract idea.

Our Creator, Father, Redeemer God

God is Creator, Father and Redeemer. Firstly, He is our God because He is our Creator:

> So God created man in his own image,
> in the image of God he created him;
> male and female he created them
> (Genesis 1:27)

Secondly, He is our God because He is our Father: "You, O Lord, are our Father" (Isaiah 63:16).

This is what the Bible calls a covenant relationship. It is not like a treaty between people or countries, when both parties agree to certain conditions. The relationship is founded on the gracious sovereign act of God – who can impose any conditions He chooses: "And God said, 'This is the sign of the covenant I am making between me and you . . . a covenant for all generations to come. I have set my rainbow in the clouds, and it will be the sign of the covenant between me and the earth" (Genesis 9:12–13).

The New Testament covenant, like that of the Old Testament, was the result of God's initiative and grace. And the price of this covenant was the blood of Jesus Christ. And Jesus Himself tells us: "This is my blood of the covenant, which is poured out for many for the forgiveness of sins" (Matthew 26:28).

Thirdly, He is our God because He is our Redeemer:

> But now, this is what the Lord says –
> he who created you, O Jacob,
> he who formed you, O Israel:
> 'Fear not, for I have redeemed you;
> I have summoned you by name; you are mine'
> (Isaiah 43:1–3)

In Bible days a ransom was the price paid to set free a slave or a prisoner. The person who paid the ransom was known as the "redeemer" and his act as one of "redemption". In the Old Testament we read of God redeeming His people from Egypt (2 Samuel 7:23), and Babylon (Jeremiah 15:21), and from national (Psalm 25:22) and personal troubles (Psalm 26:11).

This picture was carried over into the New Testament explaining our bondage as prisoners to sin (John 8:34; Romans 6:17). Here, the ransom was the sacrifice of Christ upon the cross – the price paid to set us free (Mark 10:45; 1 Peter 1:18,19).

Here are three clear statements of all that God is and has done. As Creator, Father, and Redeemer, God says, "You shall have no other gods before me." To worship any god but this Creator, Father, Redeemer God is to break this commandment. It is not necessary to worship a clearly defined god, such as Zeus or a Roman Emperor to break this commandment. We break it whenever we give some person or some thing the *first place* in our affections – which belongs to God alone. It could be music or money, a particular achievement or goal – anything that battles for first place in our lives. We need to look carefully at what takes up our time, thoughts, money, what motivates us. Are we really putting God first? The Israelites faced several dangers which can easily become dangers and pitfalls for us today, diverting and distorting our relationship with God our Father.

First danger – prosperity

When the Israelites reached the Promised Land they were faced with the temptations associated with having endless possessions:

> Be careful that you do not forget the Lord your God . . . failing to observe his commands, his laws and his decrees that I am giving you this day. Otherwise, when you eat and are satisfied, when you build fine houses and settle down, and when your herds and flocks grow large and your silver and gold increase and all you have is multiplied, then your heart will become proud and you will forget the Lord your God, who brought you out of Egypt, out of the land of slavery.
>
> (Deuteronomy 8:11–14)

Luxury and ease would blunt the edge of Israel's awareness of God. When the children of Israel had eaten, built houses and gathered possessions, it was a dangerous time. The temptation was to forget the Lord – who had given them their wealth anyway!

The Bible is full of warnings to our materialistic society. Jesus said: "You cannot serve both God and Money" (Matthew 6:24). We learn from Jesus that treasures upon earth are fleeting:

> Do not store up for yourselves treasures on earth, where moth and rust destroy, and where thieves break in and steal. But store up for yourselves treasures in heaven, where moth and rust do not destroy, and where thieves do not break in and steal. For where your treasure is, there your heart will be also.
>
> (Matthew 6:19–21)

In contrast, "the Lord will reign for ever and ever" (Exodus 15:8).

John Wesley suggested that Christians should give away all but the plain necessities of life – wholesome food, clean clothes and enough to carry on one's business. Having satisfied the necessities, the rest should be given to the poor and to God's work. He certainly lived what he preached. His books earned him £1,400 a year but he spent only £30 himself. That may be one reason why God was able to use him so powerfully to revive a decadent church and nation.

Let us be practical about the danger of prosperity and look at our own lifestyle – not at our neighbour's. Do we really need to keep up with designer fashions? Let us not be pressurised by worldly advertising and buy endless expensive toys for our children (that do not have a long life-span anyway!). Instead, let us give children more of our love and more of our time – not more things.

Second danger – pride

One of Frank Sinatra's songs is entitled "I did it my way" – the epitome of human pride. Pride is excessive self-esteem and conceit. The Israelites were warned by God about pride: "When you have eaten and are satisfied, praise the Lord your God for the good land He has given you" (Deuteronomy 8:10).

There is no one who has not been blessed by God in some area, even though they may be unaware of it and may not acknowledge God as the source. It is *God* who provides, yet we so easily forget that – as the Israelites did then. We so easily convince ourselves that something is ours because we have worked for it. But God says, "You may say to yourself, 'My power and the strength of my hands have produced this wealth for me.' But remember the Lord your God, for it is he who gives you the ability to produce wealth, and so confirms his covenant, which he swore to your forefathers, as it is today" (Deuteronomy 8:17–18).

Pride is something most of us battle with. One of the ways God works against this pride is to humble us. "Fix these words of mine in your hearts and minds; tie them as symbols on your hands and bind them on your foreheads. Teach them to your children, talking about them when you sit at home and when you walk along the road, when you lie down and when you get up. Write them on the door-frames of your houses and on your gates" (Deuteronomy 11:18–20).

We have no better example of humility than the life of Jesus here on earth. "Whoever exalts himself will be humbled, and whoever humbles himself will be exalted" (Matthew 23:12). And that is exactly what Jesus did:

He humbled himself
and became obedient to death – even death on a cross!
Therefore God exalted him to the highest place
and gave him the name that is above every name,
that at the name of Jesus every knee should bow,
in heaven and on earth and under the earth,

and every tongue confess that Jesus Christ is Lord,
to the glory of God the Father.

(Philippians 2:8–11)

Jesus found perfect peace and joy in this life of submission
and dependence upon the Father's will. He lost nothing by
giving all to God the Father. God honoured Jesus' trust and
did all for Him and Jesus humbled Himself before God.
Jesus also humbled Himself before men and made Himself
a servant. Jesus' humility was simply the surrender of
Himself to God, to allow the Father to do in Him what He
pleased – whatever men around might say or do to Him.

But we are very slow to learn this. So at times God has to
make us humble: "He humbled you, causing you to hunger
and then feeding you with manna, which neither you nor
your fathers had known, to teach you that man does not live
on bread alone but on every word that comes from the
mouth of the Lord" (Deuteronomy 8:3).

This is often painful and may make us feel discontented
and disillusioned. Trust in Him. If everything was OK and
we were completely satisfied, would we honour God? I
remember the late David Watson saying something which
has often helped me in painful learning times: "There are
some plants that produce a beautiful fragrance, but they
only produce a beautiful fragrance when crushed." We all
need to humble ourselves before the Almighty God and
feed on His truth. We need to study the Scriptures. We
could all read the Scriptures much more. If all the millions
of commuters read the Bible instead of the *Mirror*, the
Guardian, the *Sun*, *The Times*, the *Star* – would our nation
not change? Jesus is the Morning Star (Revelation 22:16).
He is the Good Shepherd (John 10:11). He is the Sun of
Righteousness (Malachi 4:2). John Henry Newman once
said: "I read the newspaper to know what people are doing
and I read the Bible to know what people ought to do."

Third danger – people

A third danger is the fear of people which, like prosperity and pride, might mean that we do not put God first. "Fear of man will prove to be a snare" (Proverbs 29:25). Pilate was afraid of Caesar (John 19). The parents of a boy healed by Jesus of blindness were afraid of the Jews (John 9:22). Felix was afraid of the Apostle Paul (Acts 24:25). Saul was afraid of the people and gave in to them (1 Samuel 15:24).

If we believe in God the Lord, we must act justly and stand up against the false god of acknowledging public opinion instead of God's truth. The early disciples said: "We must obey God rather than men!" (Acts 5:29). Many Christians were martyred because they stood for truth while other people, like the chief priests, shouted, "We have no king but Caesar" (John 19:15).

In the Old Testament book of Daniel, we have a powerful encouragement to stand in the hour of testing:

> Furious with rage, Nebuchadnezzar summoned Shadrach, Meshach and Abednego. So these men were brought before the king, and Nebuchadnezzar said to them, 'Is it true, Shadrach, Meshach and Abednego, that you do not serve my gods or worship the image of gold I have set up? Now when you hear the sound of the horn, flute . . . and all kinds of music, if you are ready to fall down and worship the image I made, very good. But if you do not worship it, you will be thrown immediately into a blazing furnace. Then what god will be able to rescue you from my hand?'
>
> (Daniel 3:13–15)

Their answer was simple: "We will not serve your gods or worship the image of gold you have set up" (Daniel 3:18).

So they were thrown into the fire. They did not know

how God would deliver them from the King – whether
they would die and be ushered into God's presence, or
whether they would be kept alive through a special act of
providence. But dead or alive they knew they were God's.

Shadrach, Meshach and Abednego were miraculously
saved. Later Nebuchadnezzar raised his eyes towards
heaven and said, "I praised the Most High; I honoured and
glorified him who lives for ever" (Daniel 4:34).

As the writer to the Hebrews says:

So we say with confidence,

> 'The Lord is my helper; I will not be afraid.
> What can man do to me?'

(Hebrews 13:6)

The most humiliating thing about going with the crowd is
that the people upon whose opinions we hang are not
usually even those whom we respect. "Do not be afraid of
any man, for judgment belongs to God" (Deuteronomy
1:17).

How do we keep this commandment?

To keep this commandment is as Jesus said: "Love the
Lord your God with all your heart and with all your soul
and with all your mind" (Matthew 22:37). In other words,
see everything from His viewpoint, make His will our guide
to light our path, and our only goal and objective to give
Him glory. It is, "to put Him first", says John Stott, "in
thought, word and deed, in business and leisure, in
friendships and career, in the use of our money, time and
talents, at work and at home". Basically it is doing things
for God's glory.

Jesus Christ is the perfect example of commandment number one. As the Apostle Paul said, "Be imitators of God, therefore" (Ephesians 5:1).

2

You shall not make for yourself an idol in the
form of anything in heaven above or on the
earth beneath or in the waters below. You shall
not bow down to them or worship them; for
I, the Lord your God, am a jealous God
punishing the children for the sin of the fathers
to the third and fourth generation of those who
hate me, but showing love to a thousand generations of those who love me and keep my
commandments.

(Exodus 20:4–6)

The problem

In the nineteenth century, Henry Martyn saw people in
India prostrating themselves before images and heard
someone tell of a vision of Jesus bowing before Moham-
med. Henry Martyn wrote: "I was cut to the soul at this
blasphemy. I could not endure existence if Jesus was not
glorified, it would be hell to me if He were also thus
dishonoured."

When the Apostle Paul arrived in Athens, he saw the city
full of idols and "was greatly distressed" (Acts 17:16). The
Greek word Paul uses can also be used to describe a heart
attack.

How is it that we can be unmoved by the fact that there
are areas of the world and nations where God is being
robbed of His glory? We have little of Henry Martyn's and
Paul's deeply felt emotion for the glory of God.

The root cause

Why do people make idols? Our God is the true and living God – He is the God who speaks. His words speak in creative power. God said, "Let there be light, and there was light" (Genesis 1:3). God has also spoken through prophets: "In the past God spoke to our forefathers through the prophets at many times and in various ways" (Hebrews 1:1). I like Ian Barclay's definition of a prophet as "someone who gushes out with what God says, therefore the basic meaning of a prophet is not someone who foretells the future, but who forth tells the Word of God". God also speaks through Jesus: "in these last days he has spoken to us by his Son" (Hebrews 1:2).

But God does *not* speak to us through artistry – as this passage from Isaiah clearly shows:

What fools they are who manufacture idols. Their hopes remain unanswered. They themselves are witnesses that this is so, for their idols neither see nor know. No wonder those who worship them are so ashamed. Who but a fool would make his own god – an idol that can help him not one whit! All that worship these will stand before the Lord in shame, along with all these carpenters – mere men – who claim that they have made a god. Together they will stand in terror. The metalsmith stands at his forge to make an axe, pounding on it with all his might. He grows hungry and thirsty, weak and faint. Then the woodcarver takes the axe and uses it to make an idol. He measures and marks out a block of wood and carves the figure of a man. Now he has a wonderful idol that can't so much as move from where it is placed. He cuts down cedars, he selects the cypress and the oak, he plants the ash in the forest to be nourished by rain. And after his care, he uses part of the wood to make a fire to warm himself and bake his bread, and then – he really does – he takes the rest of it and makes himself a god – a god for men to worship! An idol to fall down before and praise! Part of the tree he burns to roast his meat and to keep him warm and fed and well content, and with what's left he makes his god: a carved idol! He falls down before it and worships it and prays to it. 'Deliver me,' he says, 'You are my god!'

Such stupidity and ignorance! God has shut their eyes so that they cannot see, and closed their minds from understanding. The man never stops to think or figure out, 'Why, it's just a block of wood! I've burned it for heat and used it to bake my bread and roast my meat. How can the rest of it be a god? Should I fall down before a chunk of wood?' The poor, deluded fool feeds on ashes; he is trusting what can never give him any help at all. Yet he cannot bring himself to ask, 'Is this thing, this idol that I'm holding in my hand, a lie?'

(Isaiah 44:9–29, Living Bible)

When is an idol not an idol?

Before we look at what this commandment is trying to teach us, let us look at what it is not. This commandment is not a condemnation of the visual arts. It does not condemn the making of paintings and figures. In the Old Testament God tells Moses to make cherubims (Exodus 25:19), to make pomegranates (Exodus 23:33), and a lampstand in the form of a tree (Exodus 25:31).

It therefore does not mean that all the beautiful art history of the ages is idolatry. If God instructed representations of things to be made in the Old Testament, then the image is not an idol.

What this commandment is about

And so what is this commandment about? This commandment is concerned with two aspects of idolatry:
1. The worship of a false god.
2. The worship of the true God in a false way.

Worship of a false god

This commandment forbids us to worship a false god. An image becomes a false god or an idol when we attribute something spiritual to it. Therefore, the commandment does not forbid us to make images, it forbids us to make images to which we bow down. The trouble with idols is that they restrict our concept of God. If we believe we can hold God in our hands, we immediately lose sight of His power. God is "unboxable". In idolatry, we are reducing God to an extension of ourselves. So instead of worshipping the God of eternity, we are worshipping our own mental concept of God.

It is because we cannot picture God in our minds that we are tempted to create an idol. And all down through history, men have made symbols to represent the things they cannot see. God did reveal Himself fully in Jesus Christ. I find that, as I focus on the Christ of the Gospels, I do not need any other "picture" of Him. People have argued that if images help us to worship the true and living God then they have some value. Yes, but remember man's nature. Aids to worship can quickly and easily become objects of worship. The items made to help us worship God become the very things that we worship. We can see this happening to the Israelites. In Numbers 21, the Israelites were plagued with venomous snakes and the Lord said to Moses: "'Make a snake and put it up on a pole; anyone who is bitten can look at it and live.' So Moses made a bronze snake and put it up on a pole. Then when anyone was bitten by a snake and looked at the bronze snake, he lived" (Numbers 21:8–9).

The serpent was a symbol of God's healing power on which the Israelites could focus. But only those who believed God's promise would act upon the direction and live.

The brass symbol journeyed with them and the next time it appears in the Old Testament is in the Temple during King Hezekiah's reign, but now the Israelites were burning incense to the bronze snake (2 Kings 18:4). The symbol became an idol, a false god.

Worship of the true God in a false way

I always used to think that the second commandment was purely about making idols of other gods, but it also deals with our tendency to make idols of the true God and it therefore deals with the manner of our worship. In Exodus 32, while Moses was in conversation with the Lord God on Mount Sinai, the people gathered round Aaron and said:

'Come, make us gods who will go before us.' . . . Aaron answered them, 'Take off the gold earrings that your wives, your sons and your daughters are wearing and bring them to me . . .' He took what they handed him and made it into an idol cast in the shape of a calf . . . Then they said, 'These are your gods, O Israel, who brought you up out of Egypt . . .' Then the Lord said to Moses, 'Go down, because your people, whom you brought up out of Egypt, have become corrupt. They have been quick to turn away from what I commanded them and have made themselves an idol cast in the shape of a calf. They have bowed down to it . . . Now leave me alone so that my anger may burn against them that I may destroy them.'

Aaron did not think of the calf as another god. He genuinely saw it as the Lord in visible form, as is clear from the wording of the account. He identified the idol with the God who had brought the people out of Egypt (Exodus 32:4). Aaron announces its dedication with the words: "Tomorrow there will be a festival to the Lord" (Exodus 32:5). The choice of a calf may well suggest the idea of strength. But the Israelites were bringing the true, all powerful God down to the level of the impotent bull gods of Egypt. They wanted a visible representation of the living God. But God said "NO!"

What are today's idols?

We must guard against worshipping a false god and against worshipping the true God in a false way.

One idol that stands in the place of the eternal God is the god of *nationalism*: a god that is worshipped in many countries. In 1912, in Northern Ireland, a group of people entered into a pledge that there would be no home rule in Northern Ireland and made a covenant with God. But men can not initiate a covenant with God. God is the one initiator. God decides the basis on which a covenant is made – not man! Nationalism can be exalted to the point of making it a religion. People kill each other because they believe they are doing it for a god. They may be laying their lives down for nationalism, but nationalism is a false god.

There is often *denominational idolatry*. David McKee, a wonderful servant of God with whom I worked in Northern Ireland in 1979, used to say: "Our denominations are only important in the measure in which they bring us into vital contact with Jesus Christ Himself and nothing more." Have we transferred to them the loyalty that belongs to Jesus Christ alone? Some of us have lost sight of the fact that the

Church is not about structures and procedures, but about
Jesus Christ. Structures and procedures should only be
there to help us serve the true and living God. Are we
devoted to the system of rules and regulations or to Jesus
Christ?

I sometimes get highly frustrated by church rules and
regulations. One often hears, "That's not the way we do it
here." Has the way that we do things taken over from the
God for whom we should be doing these things? What is
more important – the *way* we do something or the one we
do it for – God Himself?

The history of Christianity has shown us emphasising
particular *Biblical truths* that start off right and get distorted and become idols. During these last few years there
has been a great emphasis on simple lifestyle and social
justice which are very important truths of the Christian
faith. However, for some, the truths take over and they
talk about nothing else. Do we speak and act out of anger
or do we speak and act because of the true and living
God?

We idolise *success*. We idolise *numbers*. Churches
proudly boast of their numbers. Terry Fullam, a minister in
the USA, when asked how many people were in his church
replied: "I don't know." The questioner responded, "What
do you mean you don't know?" Terry Fullam said, "Look,
the Lord didn't say count the sheep but feed them."
We happily boast about our churches' numbers, the excellence of the teaching – should we not tell people about
worshipping God?

Our world continues to idolise *materialism and money*. It
pervades all the media and as Christians we are not immune
to it. We are concerned about *status* and being known in the
right circles. *Being accepted* becomes our idol.

Worship is not only bowing down to something but
serving something – putting your life into something. Are

we serving just for some material end – work, money or pleasure – or are we serving to please God?

A jealous God?

This commandment also talks of a jealous God. How do we understand the fact that God – who is perfect, loving and holy – is also jealous? You can't have an everlasting relationship with an idol. One person and one idol does not make a love affair. An idol is a manageable substitute for the real thing and God's response to our idolatry is jealousy, just as a married person would be in hearing of their partner's affair. No rivals! You can't love a person and be tolerant of other loves. You can't love a person and be indifferent about them having affairs.

True worship means giving God the glory to which He is due. This is the purpose for which everything exists. God created the world as a theatre in which to display His glory. He created us man and woman in order to reflect the image of His glory. He sent Jesus in order that the glory of God be seen in Jesus Christ. There is *nothing* beyond this. It is the terminus of everything in the universe. He is therefore jealous for His glory. He will not give it to another.

God is jealous. The original word used literally meant "God burns". His love "glows" in jealousy. His love rages, blazes and consumes. Our disregard of God is such ingratitude, vanity and sin that it merits God's judgement. Billy Graham has said, "If God doesn't punish this modern world of sin He will have to apologise to Sodom and Gomorrah."

But at the same time as God speaks of judgement, He also speaks of having mercy upon the many generations of those who *do* love Him and keep His commandments.

If we keep looking at idols, we become like them. And

the devil knows this and tries to manipulate our minds through the media. He knows if he can get us to look at filth we will become filthy. "We become like that which we gaze upon."

Going back to continue the story of the bronze serpent, five hundred years after God gave it to Moses as a symbol, it became an idol. Hezekiah "broke into pieces the bronze snake" (2 Kings 18:4). It was an idol and it had to go. Action has to be radical. Idols must go. "Hezekiah trusted in the Lord, the God of Israel. There was no-one like him among all the Kings of Judah . . . He held fast to the Lord and did not cease to follow him; he kept the commands the Lord had given Moses. And the Lord was with him; he was successful in whatever he undertook" (2 Kings 18:5–7). God is calling us to a loyalty to Himself that supersedes all other loyalties. If we seek fulfilment from material things, we won't find it, but in seeking God we find the most fulfilling life imaginable. So let us:

> Turn our eyes upon Jesus
> Look full into His wonderful face
> And the things of earth will grow strangely dim
> In the light of that glory and grace.

3

> You shall not misuse the name of the Lord
> your God, for the Lord will not hold anyone
> guiltless who misuses his name.
>
> (Exodus 20:7)

What's in a name?

In the Old Testament, a man's soul and his name were almost indistinguishable. His whole personality was present in his name. Therefore, to know a person's name was to gain an insight into his nature and in some way acquire a relationship with him. That is why the mysterious messenger who wrestled with Jacob at Jabbok refused to disclose his name. "Jacob said, 'Please tell me your name.' But He replied, 'Why do you ask my name?'" (Genesis 32:29).

The same attitude is seen when Manoah enquired of the angel of the Lord: "'What is your name . . . ?' He replied, 'Why do you ask my name?'" (Judges 13:17–18).

A change of name indicated a deliberate and decisive change in a person's life – as when Abram becomes Abraham (Genesis 17:5), when Jacob becomes Israel (Genesis 32:28) and, later, in the New Testament, when Saul becomes Paul (Acts 13:9).

In the Old Testament, to have done something in someone's name or to call upon their name were actions of the utmost seriousness. To call on a person's name was to make them effectively present. Understanding this helps us to

grasp the meaning of many passages related to this commandment. The Orthodox Jews thought that the name of
God was so sacred that when they were writing His name
with quills, they would immediately throw them away and
use a new quill. And when they were reading the Old
Testament Scripture and came to the name of God, they
would not pronounce it. We may be amused by this, but
they had an immense awe and reverence for the name of
God.

What about us? A lot of us do not appreciate the real
value of God's name. God's name has real value and
worth. The significance of God's name must be looked at in
two ways – its significance to God and its significance to us.
In other words, we must look at what it shows us about God
and how that should affect our behaviour.

The name of God

God's name is a revelation of His glory. The name of God
represents the nature of God. To know His name is to know
of His existence. The names of God reveal something of
His character. The various names of God represent His
many praiseworthy attributes.

The different names of God have specific meanings.
Elohim means "the Creator of all that is". It is the name
used in the opening verse of the Bible: "In the beginning
Elohim (God) created the heavens and the earth" (Genesis
1:1). El Elyon means "God the Most High". This name
emphasises God's rule and Sovereignty. Melchizedek was
"priest of El Elyon (God Most High)" (Genesis 14:18). In
Exodus, we read the story of Moses and the burning bush:
Yahweh is "I AM THAT I AM". It speaks of God's self-
existence and eternity. It is also used in God's revelations
of Himself as Redeemer.

The Old Testament understanding of the name passes from the Old Testament into the New. The names of our Lord Jesus Christ reveal His character, worth and work. The name Jesus means Saviour. It is a very special and precious name. Men are healed and evil spirits are cast out through the name of Jesus (Matthew 7:22). The name of Jesus carries power. It is the authority by which the Holy Spirit comes (John 14:26). It is the authority for salvation (Romans 10:13) and baptism (Matthew 28:19).

The Apostle Paul wrote:

Therefore God exalted him (Jesus) to the highest place
and gave him the name that is above every name,
that at the name of Jesus every knee should bow,
in heaven and on earth and under the earth,
and every tongue confess that Jesus Christ is Lord,
to the Glory of God the Father.

(Philippians 2:9–11)

Once we appreciate the power of Jesus' name, we will have a fuller understanding of many familiar passages: The Lord's Prayer, "Hallowed be your name" (Matthew 6:9); Christ's promise at the Last Supper, "I tell you the truth, my Father will give you whatever you ask in my name" (John 16:23); His final command, "Go and make disciples of all nations, baptising them in the name of the Father and of the Son and of the Holy Spirit" (Matthew 28:19).

When do we take His name in vain?

Many Christians Sunday by Sunday stand up in church and make a confession of their belief. The confession is known as the Apostles' Creed. It starts: "I believe in God, the Father Almighty, Creator of heaven and earth." Martin

Luther met a man weeping by the roadside and enquired what was the problem. The man told emotionally of how his house, his property, his wealth had been burnt down the night before. Luther asked him if he knew the Creed. He said "Yes" and Luther requested the man to recite it. "I believe in God, the Father Almighty, Creator of heaven and earth." Luther said, "Stop, would you please repeat it." "I believe in God, the Father Almighty, Creator of heaven and earth." And Luther said, "Well, that's it then, if you really believe that you've got nothing to worry about."

Do we honour him as Sovereign God? If we do not honour Him by respecting His names, we break His commandment. If we doubt His ability to care for us and keep His promises and complain about circumstances, then we do not honour Him as Sovereign God. The Psalmist said, "I will declare your name" (Psalm 22:22), expressing that he desires to speak about all that God is. When we use one of His names in an empty, negative context we are degrading Him. Not only is His name significant to Him, but it should be so for us.

My wife's name is Killy – it is precious to me. Killy is the name of someone I love very much. If people used my wife's name casually and flippantly, it would concern me. In just the same way, it should concern us when God's name is used by people, including Christians, in a callous way. If we treat His name as nothing, this commandment teaches us that God "will not hold anyone guiltless" when we do so.

The Israelites often took vows and there was nothing wrong with that. In their vows they would often use the name of God: "I swear by the Lord that . . ." (2 Samuel 19:7). There was nothing wrong – if you meant it. If you said it acknowledging the seriousness of involving the Holy God Almighty in your vows, it was acceptable. However, to have used the name of God without any significance was

a serious violation of His name. We must not be too quick
to make promises to God unless we mean to go through
with them. We sometimes say "Lord, if you do this then I
promise I'll stop doing that and do this." Let us never
say more with our lips than can be validated with our
actions.

> Lord, who may dwell in your sanctuary?
> He . . .
> who keeps his oath
> even when it hurts.
>
> (Psalm 15:1,4)

> I will come to your temple with burnt offerings
> and fulfil my vows to you –
> vows my lips promised and my mouth spoke
> when I was in trouble.
>
> (Psalm 66:13–14)

Many today swear in everyday conversation. "Do not
swear falsely by my name" (Leviticus 19:12). If we get
angry, it can be "Jesus Christ". If we hear bad news, "Oh
God". If we want to persuade someone, "For heaven's
sake". If we have forgotten something, "Oh Lord". Expressions such as "For God's sake" are often used as verbal
exclamation points.

Even expressions like "Hallelujah" and "Praise the
Lord" are thrown about with such frequency that they
become empty religious phrases – for us, not for God. In
one place where I was staying, during breakfast one of the
hosts said, "Pass the toast over, praise the Lord." I should
not have allowed the statement to pass without counteract-
ing the dishonour of God's name. We often hear people
say, when rebuked, "That's not swearing – I didn't mean it

disrespectfully. I could just have said 'damn'. I didn't mean anything by it." EXACTLY. To take God's name in vain so it means nothing is breaking the third commandment.

We can easily misuse the name of God to manipulate a situation if we think that it will further our cause. For example, if we ask someone to do something and they react with a great deal of uncertainty and hesitancy, we can be quick to suggest, "Well, ask the Lord to show you in prayer." Is this the right use of God's name? Or are we trying to spiritualise a situation by using God's name? The classic example is when one person tells someone, "I believe the Lord wants us to get married", which I gather has often happened to Cliff Richard!

We take God's name in vain when we use it as an item for humour and entertainment. This is not to say that we should not laugh. It is healthy to laugh at ourselves, but when unbelievers mock Him and His name on television and radio, do we *just* laugh along with everybody else or do we feel hurt because we honour God and His name? Do we stand in awe of His name? (Malachi 2:5).

More than words . . . our "behaviour"

We take His name in vain when we dishonour the name Christian. Those of us who belong to God have, in a sense, taken His name, and we must hallow it by our actions. If we "commit adultery" with the world, we transgress against His love and dishonour the name Christian – which means "a Christ one". We act fraudulently when our behaviour does not match our beliefs. Judas Iscariot believed in Jesus Christ, but his behaviour did not correspond to that belief. We disgrace the name of the Lord when our practice does not match what we claim to believe. When Jesus saw the Pharisees He said, quoting Isaiah:

These people honour me with their lips,
but their hearts are far from me.
They worship me in vain;
their teachings are but rules taught by men.
(Matthew 15:8–9)

Jesus demands more than words from the lips, he also
demands a commitment from our hearts so that the words
can be put into practice. We dishonour the name of God if
we profess to be that which we are not. We are then
hypocrites and "God's name is blasphemed among the
Gentiles because of you" (Romans 2:24). "They claim to
know God, but by their actions they deny Him. They are
detestable, disobedient and unfit for doing anything good"
(Titus 1:16).

As Christians we take the name of Christ, so the way we
behave reflects what we think of God.

The therapeutic approach

Another way we take God's name in vain has been growing
through a psychological school of thought. This basically
says that we are to be honest with God and that honesty
involves telling Him exactly what you think in whatever
way you choose – this apparently releases you and relieves
you of anger and frustration. The upshot of this school's
teaching is that we can shout at God, swear at God and call
Him names.

The Biblical basis put forward in support of this therapeutic approach is in the Psalms – which are full of accounts
of similar activity of throwing resentment and anger against
God.

Whatever the value of this theory, it is not based on a
proper understanding of the Bible. Just because a human's

reaction is there in Scripture, it does not mean it is to be imitated. In the book of Job, we read that his wife said to him, "'Are you still holding on to your integrity? Curse God and die!'" (Job 2:9). These examples are illustrations and not doctrine – therefore we should take it as such. The Bible records many wrong human reactions as well as right ones. God does not allow His commandments to be broken for therapeutic purposes. The Psalmist says, "When my heart was grieved and my spirit embittered, I was senseless and ignorant; I was a brute beast before you" (Psalm 73:21–22). In other words, "the things I said to you were foolish and evil and therefore they should never have been said". Of course, we must talk to our heavenly Father with honesty, but also with respect.

So let us not be like those Orthodox Jews and treat God's name as so sacred that we do not mention it, but let us learn to love His names and what they stand for. Let us stand up for His name when it is dishonoured.

> Give thanks to the Lord, call on his name;
> make known among the nations what he has done.
> Sing to him, sing praise to him;
> tell of all his wonderful acts.
> Glory in his holy name;
> let the hearts of those who seek the Lord rejoice.
> Look to the Lord and his strength;
> seek his face always.
>
> (Psalm 105:1–4)

4

> Remember the Sabbath day by keeping it holy.
> Six days you shall labour and do all your work
> but the seventh day is a Sabbath to the Lord
> your God. On it you shall not do any work,
> neither you, nor your son or daughter, nor
> your manservant or maidservant, nor your
> animals, not the alien within your gates. For in
> six days the Lord made the heavens and the
> earth, the sea and all that is in them, but He
> rested on the seventh day. Therefore the Lord
> blessed the Sabbath day and made it holy.
>
> (Exodus 20:8)

There is more disagreement over the meaning of this commandment than of any other. To some people, it is irrelevant and restrictive, but others believe it is important and endeavour to obey it wholeheartedly. It can be confusing – and difficult to discover what God is really saying to us. But we need to be prepared for God to challenge us on everything in relation to the Sabbath.

A positive, vital, necessary commandment

This commandment starts positively. It isn't a "Thou Shalt Not" commandment – it begins with "Remember". From the moment of creation God intended and required us to observe a day of rest. The Sabbath is not an afterthought. It is just as important as the other nine commandments. God is saying that, because He loves us, He has given us one day in seven to stop us working seven days a week. This commandment protects us as human beings. Remember when the Israelites were slaves under Pharaoh and had to provide bricks *every day*? The commandment stresses that human beings are people who need to have a break at least one day in seven. In the nineteenth century, Brook Herford wrote, "I think the world of today would go mad, just frenzied with strain and pressure, but for the blessed institution of Sunday."

The fourth commandment is a fundamental part of God's Law for sound living. However, despite this, it is true that we break this commandment more often than the others – or we more obviously break it. We find that more and more things happen on Sunday than used to.

The evangelist D. L. Moody, preaching a sermon in 1880, was lamenting the fact that people were no longer observing Sunday as they did:

> You want power in your Christian life do you? You want Holy Ghost power? You want the dew of heaven on your brow? You want to see men convicted and converted? I don't believe that we will ever have any genuine conversions until we get straight on this law of God. Men seem to think that they have a right to change a Holy day into a holiday and nowadays young Christians have more temptations to break the Sabbath than we had 40 years ago in 1840. You show me a nation that has given up the Sabbath and I will show you a nation that has got seeds of decay.

Reading Moody's sermon, we realise that we are even further down the line than he was then. He was concerned about the fact that trains and buses were starting to run on a

Sunday. Most of us have accepted trains and buses running on a Sunday since the day we were born. The problem we have with this commandment is that each generation accepts more and more – and Sunday becomes less and less a holy day.

There is a great danger that we accept things in our materialistic world simply because we have always known them to be like that. However, through this command-ment, God asks us to question our ways of going about things. He asks us to take a long, hard look at everything that was established as normal practice before we were born – and that is a very big challenge. We challenge the way that laws allow abortion because we believe that it puts God's standard at stake. But what about such practices as treating Sunday much the same as any other day?

Some of you may be thinking, "But through Christ's death, we've entered into the freedom of the Spirit. We don't want to get bogged down in keeping the Sabbath day holy. It was the cause of so much legalism in the church in the past." In no sense are we wanting to bring back legalism. However, I believe that Moody was right when he said that every command of God is there to be obeyed, and unless we obey them we will not have spiritual power.

What day is the Sabbath?

Before we go any further in unpacking this commandment, we need to sort out what often seems to be a problem with it. The problem is that the Sabbath in the Old Testament was the seventh day of the week which is our Saturday, but now as Christians we observe Sunday – the first day of the week.

Many people cannot avoid working on Sunday – for example, police and nurses. Are they breaking the fourth commandment? No, for them the key is to do six days' work and keep the seventh as a day of rest – so one in seven is a day off. If we understand that the provision of the day is to do with God's love, we can see there is no particular sanctity in it being on the seventh or the first. There is of course great value when Christians meet together for worship – on the same day! There is value in worshipping on the same day as a practicality – but when that isn't possible, the principle is that one in seven should be a day off.

People who argue that the Sabbath has to be Saturday cannot do so from the Bible or from early Christian history. The Jewish people actually forced the first Christians out of the synagogues and when the Gentiles (the non-Jewish people who became Christians) joined, they had to move their corporate worship to the evening after the Sabbath. In the third century, Christianity began to have an influence on the Government of the day. Eventually through the Emperor Constantine, its constitution changed and required one day off in seven to enable people to worship. It was a holy day. The practice of resting on the first day of the week was established and Sunday worship became the norm for Christians. The first day of the week was also the day Jesus rose from the dead – a central day of the Christian calendar. The Apostle Paul clearly avoids and warns against any kind of legalistic attitude to any particular day: "Therefore do not let anyone judge you by what you eat or drink, or with regard to a religious festival, a New Moon celebration or a Sabbath day" (Colossians 2:16). The apostle tells us not to be concerned about which day it is and says, "The reality, however, is found in Christ" (Colossians 2:17).

If a particular day is convenient for us to come together and worship Him, then of course we will endeavour to keep that day together. It does not matter which day it is.

Six days you shall labour – but not seven

The commandment instructs us that the Sabbath is a day of rest and a day dedicated to God (Exodus 20:11). A day of rest was the Lord's pattern in creation: "By the seventh day God had finished the work he had been doing; so on the seventh day he rested from all his work. And God blessed the seventh day and made it holy, because on it he rested from all the work of creating that he had done" (Genesis 2:2–3). "Remember six days you shall labour." Sometimes we need to emphasise this part of the commandment. Resting on the seventh day is dependent on the six working days. This is *not* a condemnation on those who are unemployed. Those who are unemployed need to use the six days as profitably as possible. Most people have more than one day off in seven and many of us today work fewer hours than people in previous centuries. We have weekends, extra holidays at Christmas and Easter and summer holidays. So part of the purpose of rest and refreshment is being enjoyed by many of us to the full. If we fail to take a day of rest, we go against our Creator's best intention, basically saying to God "I know better". Most of us can take Saturday and Sunday off from our normal weekly work. Saturday gives us an opportunity to do other work – around the house, on the car, etc. But we need to take care. Those who are self-employed may have a great temptation to work seven days a week. Don't. *Disobeying* God's guidelines can only be harmful.

Students may be in danger of working seven days a week, thus going against God's instructions. If you do that, you will be a poorer student with a real danger of being slowed down by exhaustion. Take a clear day off and as Michael Baughen, now Bishop of Chester, used to do when he was a student – on Sundays, laugh at the books and enjoy the liberty that they do not need opening.

Sir James Crichton-Browne commented: "We doctors, in the treatment of nervous diseases are now constantly compelled to prescribe periods of rest. Some periods are, I think, only Sundays in arrears."

Osborne House on the Isle of Wight was one of Queen Victoria's houses. When she first arrived on the island to take up residence it was Saturday. All the local tradesmen wanted the business of the Royal household and, on Sunday, they all sent up their servants and foremen with their cards and said they hoped Her Majesty would appoint them as her suppliers. On the Monday morning, the Queen looked at all the cards and said to her servant, "Are all the cards of all the local tradesmen here?" "No, your Majesty," he said, "There is one card missing – from the large grocer in the village." Queen Victoria asked why the card was not there. The servant replied, "I contacted him, but he said he wouldn't send his card in on a Sunday." Queen Victoria immediately said, "That's the man I want to supply groceries for the Royal household."

The outward keeping of the Sabbath will be a sign that we regard God as Creator and Saviour. Christian workers, as I am, must also take special note of these warnings and not allow themselves to fall into continuous work, straining their capabilities and relationships.

It's worth recognising that this is the only commandment that deals with family, servants and animals, as well as ourselves (Exodus 20:8–10). We must therefore take the responsibility for "making" others work. Few of us have servants today, but we are servants of our own households. So, for our own benefit, we need to minimise the chores – cleaning and cooking – on at least one day of the week. If possible, prepare Sunday lunch on Saturday. Think and act wisely and be free on the Sabbath.

Something positive – what should we do?

The Sabbath is a day of rest and a day *dedicated to God*.
"Therefore the Lord blessed the Sabbath day and made it
holy" (Exodus 20:11). Blessing means a "pool of water" –
an oasis in our desert world. As well as a blessing, the
Sabbath should be a recreation of mind, body and soul. As
one of the Puritans put it, it is "the market day of the soul".
Someone said: "It's a day for our souls to catch up with our
bodies." God also made it "holy". He "hallowed" it, He
set it. The emphasis is on what *we do do*, rather than what
we do not do.

It was Jesus' custom to go to the synagogue on the
Sabbath (Luke 4:16). The worship at the synagogue must
often have suffered from a formalism and deadness that He
must have found distressing, but He went all the same.
Likewise, we should join in God's family worshipping Him
on His day. The day is not cancelled simply because we may
feel bored with the worship and feel that it does us no good.
*It is to God and not to ourselves that we are making an
offering in our worship*.

There are three references in the New Testament to the
Christian celebration of the Lord's Day. Two of them refer
to public worship. On the first day of the week, the disciples
came together to celebrate the Lord's Supper (Acts 20:7).
Also, the Apostle Paul encouraged the Corinthians to be
financially generous on the Sabbath (1 Corinthians 16:2).

In 1924, during the Olympic Games, a Christian called
Eric Liddell had a preliminary draw on the Sabbath. He
refused to run, casting doubt about his loyalty to his king
and country and a certain imbalance in his mind. He was
subsequently moved from the 100 metres race to the 400
metres race. Just before he began the race someone quoted
a verse to him: "Those who honour me I will honour" (1
Samuel 2:30). He ran. He won and he broke the world

record for the 400 metres. The story is told graphically in
the award-winning film *Chariots of Fire*.

The example of Jesus

Finally, let us look at how Jesus dealt with this question of
observing the Sabbath.

> One Sabbath Jesus was going through the cornfields, and
> as His disciples walked along, they began to pick some
> ears of corn. The Pharisees said to Him, 'Look, why are
> they doing what is unlawful on the Sabbath?' He
> answered, 'Have you never read what David did when he
> and his companions were hungry and in need? In the days
> of Abiathar the high priest, he entered the house of God
> and ate the consecrated bread, which is lawful only for
> priests to eat. And he also gave some to his companions.'
> Then He said to them, 'The Sabbath was made for man
> and not man for the Sabbath. So the Son of Man is Lord
> even of the Sabbath.'
>
> (Mark 2:23–28)

In the time of Jesus the Scribes and Pharisees took what was
a good Law of God – the Sabbath Law – and hemmed it in
with petty regulations. That made the Sabbath a burden, so
Jesus took issue with it. Jesus said that the Sabbath is not a
burden. Sabbath was made for man's good. It is God's Law
– but we must not be stupid with it, we must understand its
true meaning.

In Matthew 12 we are told that Jesus allowed works of
necessity on the Sabbath. "If an ox needs a drink then lead
it to water." Secondly, he allowed works of emergency. "If
an ass falls into a pit you don't say 'I'll come tomorrow.'"
Just as, if our chimney is on fire we do not say we will ring

the Fire Brigade on Monday. Thirdly, he allowed works of mercy. It is obvious we should do works of mercy and goodness. It is obviously right to visit a sick person. Jesus says we must be sensible. The great danger is that when Jesus says we must be sensible – we say "oh yes" and therefore include everything under that heading.

Jesus allows works of necessity.

Jesus allows works of emergency.

Jesus allows works of mercy.

These things are in fact exceptions to the general rule that we stop work on a Sabbath.

An Old Testament illustration

There is a Law in the Old Testament that when the Children of Israel came into the Promised Land as a nation they were told: "Give a Sabbath rest to the land every seven years." One year in every seven do not work the land, and if you keep that law you will receive as much in six years as you would in seven. For 490 years the people of Israel disobeyed the command. They were then taken into exile by Nebuchadnezzar. When they were in exile, out of the land of Israel, they were obviously receiving no produce from the land.

For how many years? 70.

Note: 7×70 years = 490.

They were told by God to give a Sabbath year every seven – but they did not and God took it back from them. I believe that this picture is very important for us. If we do not give the Sabbath to God, He will take it. The blessing that God wants to give may not come.

5

Honour your father and your mother, so that
you may live long in the land the Lord your
God is giving you.

(Exodus 20:12)

A positive commandment

This commandment is a positive focus on the smallest unit
of society – the family – which is fundamental to all other
social relationships and structures. It is a commandment
that does not contain a negative. A child is not to grow up in
the negative environment of "You are not to disobey your
parents", but in the positive environment, "honour your
mother and father". The training of children does not begin
with a series of negatives but with one positive.

An urgent commandment

This is the only commandment that does not last a lifetime.
It is different from all the other commandments in that the
other nine are instructions we should obey until we die.
However, for most of us – although not for all of us – the
opportunity to obey *this* commandment ends when our
parents die. There may come a time when we can no longer
give the honour to our parents as God commands. This is
therefore an urgent commandment – for when our parents

die it is too late. A day may come when we will not be able
to make amends.

Some people's parents may have died and they may have
sensed a serious violation of this commandment only subsequently. If so, we can be assured of God's forgiveness
and the assurance that He will not hold it against us. "As far
as it depends on you, live at peace with everyone" (Romans
12:18). So if you have now recognised wrong attitudes
towards your parents, then "as much as it lies in you",
forgive your parents, receive forgiveness from God and
forgive yourself. Then honour your parents in speech with
an uncritical spirit. Never speak badly of them, for you
have been forgiven by God and God does not hold your sins
against you. So in forgiving your parents you should not
hold their sins against them.

A commandment with a promise

This is the only commandment with a promise. All the
commandments hold implicit promises, but this is the only
commandment with a specific promise. The commandment
promises a lifetime of blessing – "so that you may live long
in the land the Lord your God is giving you". God is
showing how central to a wholesome life the theme of
honouring one's parents is. This commandment also suggests that there is something unhealthy about children –
and consequently adults – who fail to honour their parents.
It is not part of God's natural design and therefore it will
inevitably affect us deep down.

Good families make a healthy society. This is a very
important truth – particularly in times when some people
have said and continue to say that the family is not very
important. Scholars believe that the original meaning of
this commandment was that we should care for our parents

when they are growing old. The logic behind this interpretation is that no Jewish eleven-year-old would need to be told, "honour your parents", because he or she would already be doing so. It would be like saying to a Jewish child, "breathe" – they do. In Jewish society, children would readily and naturally honour their parents by obeying and respecting them. It would not occur to them to do anything else. Today's society is a different matter.

God's family relationships are to be built on love and trust – love and trust between the parents and the child, the giving and receiving of love and trust. But often today, the marriage breaks up and creates problems in obeying this command. One in three marriages breaks up and nine out of ten divorcees remarry. We are inevitably fractured if our father and mother no longer love each other. Often there is a great deal of tension, bitterness and resentment. It is therefore very difficult to know how to honour and to be able to love where there has ceased to be love. A new love, with a new stepmother or stepfather, can be equally disturbing.

Obedience to this commandment is vital to healthy growth in life. If the growing child does not have a loving, respectful relationship with one's parents, because of a break-up in marriage, he or she is deprived of a basic need. There is a promise in Scripture that the Lord can replace that distorted, absent love. Jesus says, "I will not leave you as orphans; I will come to you" (John 14:18).

"Leave your orphans; I will protect their lives. Your widows too can trust in me" (Jeremiah 49:11). The Lord *can* heal. You may be approaching this commandment with real suspicion and hesitancy because, for some reason, you have not experienced the joys of a fulfilling parental relationship. That is why it is vital to know that God is "Our Father" (Matthew 6:9). When we become members of the family of God, we often find that we need our heavenly

Father's healing, forgiveness, blessing and love in areas to do with this commandment.

How do we honour our parents?

According to the Anglican Catechism, this commandment means, "To love our parents, honour our parents and succour our parents." Calvin wrote, "This commandment means we should look up to those whom God has placed over us and treat them with honour, obedience and gratefulness." My thesaurus contains the following words for "honour" – "reverence, respect, obedience, gratitude, trust, confidence, praise, attention, esteem, adore, consideration and care". These words reflect what honour means in the context of this commandment at the various stages of our development.

Trust and obedience

If children are not taught to respect their parents, and are allowed to get away with disobeying and dishonouring them, later in life they are more likely to rebel against other valid forms of authority. If they do not respect their parents, they may not respect their teachers. If they do not obey their parents, they may not obey the laws of the land. If they do not obey their parents, will they honour God?

In 1968 the United Nations produced a Charter of Children's Rights. The document details all the rights that children should have, protecting them from exploitation. It is an excellent document, but what it doesn't include is a right for parents or guardians to discipline the children – this right is fundamental to the teaching of the Bible.

> Train a child in the way he should go,
> and when he is old he will not turn from it.
> (Proverbs 22:6)

> Discipline your son, for in that there is hope;
> do not be a willing party to his death.
> (Proverbs 19:18)

Proverbs again advises us:

> He who spares the rod hates his son,
> but he who loves him is careful to discipline him.
> (Proverbs 13:24)

As parents, we will of course be more effective in disciplining our children when we also have their respect. We gain their respect when we "practise what we preach", when we spend time with them. We must not neglect our children. To us fathers – the care and teaching of children is not just women's work! Joy Davidman, in her book *Smoke on the Mountain*, says, "rearing a family is far more real and rewarding than making and spending money". Of course, money is necessary, but working all the hours of the day may not prove to be the best way to become whole and healthy. It is parents – good parents – that children need. Abraham Lincoln used to say, "All that I have I owe to my mother."

My wife Killy and I find that there is a real challenge to be consistent. We must correct our children, whether in private or in public. If we are inconsistent in our discipline, then they will not know whether they are coming or going. Remember – they are filled with original sin!

Martin Luther comments, "Spare the rod and spoil the child that is true. But beside the rod keep an apple to give him when he's done well." That is an important lesson. If parents are to expect obedience, they must encourage that obedience. The Bible admonishes children to honour their parents. On the other hand, it has an equally serious word for parents: "Fathers, do not exasperate your children; instead, bring them up in the training and instruction of the Lord" (Ephesians 6:4). Parents must not provoke their children and, as Luther suggests, we must not be discouraging. We need to encourage. Constant encouragement is a quality that abounds in Jewish families. We must be careful to build children up and not put them down, for the child may easily become totally discouraged and may obey out of fear – not out of love and respect.

In the Old Testament, the family was a basic unit not only in society but also in religion. It was not the duty of the priest in the Old Testament to teach the children. Today we tend to think that it is the duty of the Sunday School teacher to teach our children about faith – but it is not. Sunday School teachers give invaluable assistance, but the parents are the key. "In the future, when your son asks you, 'What is the meaning of the stipulations, decrees and laws the Lord our God has commanded us?' tell him . . ." (Deuteronomy 6:20–21). This is something my wife and I enjoy sharing with our children. We have always prayed for them and with them daily – even before they were born! We have always had prayers and Bible reading after breakfast. When our son Michael was about two, he began to take an active part and have his own "quiet time" before bedtime (with Simon and Sarah notes!). Now sometimes when we are absolutely exhausted and are particularly keen to put him to bed, he is the one who reminds us about the "quiet time".

Gratitude and respect

We should *respect the experience* that our parents have gained. We should also *acknowledge the sacrifice* that our parents have made. The first years of a child's life are frail. Parents make sacrifices in order to care, nurse, feed and clothe. Babies cannot survive by themselves. We should respect our parents for what they have done. The adolescent period of development is perhaps the most difficult time in relating to parents, because teenagers have many new ideas and feel that their parents are behind the times and ignorant. Mark Twain wrote: "When I was fourteen my father was so ignorant I could hardly bear him, but by the time I was twenty-one I was amazed to see how much he had learned in seven years." Of course, Mark Twain's father had not changed at all. In those seven years Mark Twain had developed into a position where he could respect and honour his father. At fourteen he was only thinking of himself.

In Luke's Gospel we have a glimpse of Jesus at the beginning of His teenage years. It is the first account where Jesus Himself acknowledges who He is. Jesus says to His mother Mary and earthly father, "Didn't you know I had to be in my Father's house?" (Luke 2:49). In other words, at the age of twelve, the beginning of His adolescent years, Jesus realised who He was and who His Father was. He was the Son of God and His real Father was in heaven.

Jesus realised how great He was. This is often the root of the problem for parents of a teenage child. As the teenager begins to realise – or believe – how great he or she is, seeds of disrespect begin to grow. For this reason, this glimpse of Jesus at twelve years old is particularly important and significant – we see His reaction to His parents' concern. "Then he (Jesus) went down to Nazareth with them and was obedient to them . . . And Jesus grew in wisdom and stature and found favour with God and men" (Luke 2:51–52). Jesus was *obedient* to them. He gave them gratitude and respect. He grew and found "favour *with* God and men".

Jesus said to Mary and Joseph, "Didn't you know?" (Luke 2:49). Nevertheless, He showed Mary and Joseph the respect and honour of going home with them and being obedient. It is important not only for the child but for parents that there should be this honour. Mary was clearly enriched by what Jesus said and did – "His mother treasured all these things in her heart" (Luke 2:51).

We can honour parents by *being open* with them. It is one of the things they really appreciate. Do they know about our friends and ambitions? We often feel that our parents will not understand so we never talk to them about them. In doing this we undermine their wisdom and concern and, consequently, parents are hurt and even suspicious because nothing is said.

The book of Judges records the story of Samson. Samson could hardly be described as a "mummy's boy". Samson was asked about the meaning of a certain riddle. He replied: "I haven't even explained it to my father or mother . . . so why should I explain it to you?" (Judges 14:16). He suggests that his parents are among the first people he will confide in. When children confide in parents, parents must not use it as fuel for amusing conversation in public! It can undermine the trust placed in parents.

We can also honour our parents by *expressing warmth and affection* for them. In the Old Testament we read about Elisha – the man who was a model leader (all in 2 Kings). When Elijah anointed Elisha as prophet, his first reaction was: "Let me kiss my father and mother goodbye" (1 Kings 19:20).

We tend to feel that it is childish to *show affection* to our parents. As we get older, we gradually become more and more self-conscious. We abandon affection in most revealing ways – like deliberately walking round some piece of furniture to avoid any motherly affection. When there is no physical contact, the relationship can grow cold. Surely part of honouring our parents is to love them and part of loving them is, like Elisha, to show them affection.

If this dimension has ceased in the relationship and now seems really unnatural, start today – be bold! Just introduce it naturally with a hug and a kiss. There must be very few parents who would not feel honoured.

Now the difficulty from the parents' side is that they can be too possessive and not allow growing freedom to their children. In that environment, it makes it difficult for the young person to give gratitude and respect, unless parents are willing to allow that person to become a separate individual.

One of the problems I find – and I'm married with two children – is that my parents still treat me like a little boy. They still moan about my hairstyle and clothes. This exasperates me! If we are going to encourage children to honour and respect their parents, then parents must have the right attitude to their children, which will encourage obedience to that command.

Esteem and consideration

This is particularly relevant when we leave home as students or leave home for work. We need to show consideration for our parents – to think carefully about them; to show esteem for them – to have great respect and high regard for them. We must be careful not to despise them. We must be careful how we speak about our parents to other people. Do we speak in such a manner that implies disrespect? Do we talk of our father as "the old man"? Disrespect is a great danger for me as my parents did not approve of me becoming a Christian and an evangelist, they did not approve of my marriage and did not attend our wedding. There is a danger of speaking about them disre-

spectfully and making judgements. But we are reminded by
Jesus, "Do not judge, or you too will be judged" (Matthew
7:1). That does not mean I cannot talk about how I feel
about everything. But talking about it with friends and
family should not become an excuse for gossip.

We can show consideration and esteem for them by
visiting them regularly. If we hardly ever visit our parents,
we are saying that we value them very little, that they do not
mean much to us. Of course, some of us may be restricted
by circumstances if we live in a different country from our
parents. We could write or telephone regularly. We need,
of course, to build a new life in the new situation that God
has led us to – but we must keep honouring our parents and
that includes consideration. After my wife Killy and I got
married we telephoned my parents once a week and visited
them once a month. This wasn't always easy but we felt for
us that it was necessary.

Esteem and consideration also includes *respecting their
advice*. Proverbs encourages us: "Listen, my sons, to a
father's instruction" (Proverbs 4:1); "Do not forsake your
mother's teaching" (Proverbs 6:20). We think we know
best – which is arrogant. We cannot imagine our parents
having anything worthwhile to say. We often feel there is
no point even listening to our parents if they are not
Christians. Wrong. Their credentials are still good. They
know us. They have a longer experience of life.

*Does respecting advice imply total acceptance and
obedience to it?*

"Children, obey your parents in everything, for this pleases
the Lord" (Colossians 3:20). When our parents' advice, or
wishes, are in *direct* opposition to the will of God, we do not
obey them. Jesus said: "If anyone comes to me and does
not hate his father and mother, his wife and children, his

brothers and sisters – yes, even his own life – he cannot be my disciple" (Luke 14:26). This is strong language but Jesus was *not* commanding us to hate our families, but showing that devotion to one's family must take second place to devotion to Christ. Of course you do not obey them if they ask you to lie. Of course you do not obey them if your parents try to marry you off to some unbelieving partner – which my parents did to me!

We must *not*, however, use our faith as an excuse to get out of family commitments. Look up Mark 7:9–13. Maybe going to a church houseparty instead of a major family get-together is based on inadequate grounds that we must put God first!

In understanding this word "obey", it is helpful to look a little at Jewish culture. Children were brought up to obey their parents, but there was a decisive moment of change: "For this reason a man will leave his father and mother and be united to his wife and they will become one flesh" (Genesis 2:24). This means that, once married, they are not to run to their parents first when seeking advice. They are first to consult their partner for advice. First and foremost, married couples are bound to each other – not to their parents. Married couples are to consult each other's wishes. This, of course, was written for married couples. What about single adults? Are they to obey their parents?

In the book of Numbers we have the regulations the Lord gave Moses concerning relationships (Numbers 30). A child and a youth should obey their parents. A married person looks to the partner. A widow or divorced person is not bound to anyone. The Israelites knew no gap between living at home with one's parents and marriage – as many of us do today. There are many single people who are no longer living with their parents. It seems from Scriptures that when we are no longer living with our parents, we are released from parental authority – as the widow and divorced person. A student at college has not necessarily left home! There are parental obligations – as there are with all of us.

Care and attention

One of the things that happened in pagan society to people who had grown old and were no longer useful was that they were thrown away – literally. They were thrown onto the rubbish heap. God's command is to honour our parents. That involves *care and attention* – especially when they are growing old. We must look after them and treat them with courtesy when they can no longer look after themselves. Another story from Joy Davidman's *Smoke on the Mountain*: "Once upon a time there was a little old man. His eyes blinked and his hands trembled. When he ate he clattered the silverware distressingly, missed his mouth with the spoon as often as not and dribbled a bit of his food on the tablecloth. Now he lived with his married son, having nowhere else to live and his son's wife was a modern young woman who knew that in-laws should not be tolerated in a woman's home. 'I can't have this,' she said, 'it interferes with a woman's right to happiness.'

"So she and her husband took the little old man gently but firmly by the arm and led him to the corner of the kitchen. There they sat him on a stool and gave him his food. One day his hands trembled rather more than usual and the earthenware bowl fell and broke. 'If you are a pig', said the daughter-in-law, 'you must eat out of a trough.' So they made him a little wooden trough and he got his meals in that.

"These people had a four-year-old son of whom they were very fond. One supper time the young man noticed

his boy playing intently with some bits of wood and asked
him what he was doing.

" 'I'm making a trough,' he said, smiling up for approval,
'to feed you and mamma out of when I get big.'

"The man and his wife looked at each other for a while
and didn't say anything. Then they cried a little. Then they
went to the corner and took the little old man by the arm
and led him back to the table. They sat him in a comfortable
chair and gave him his food on a plate, and from then on
nobody ever scolded him when he clattered or spilled or
broke things."

Honouring our parents means caring for them and
attending to them. If we do not, our children will not
honour us in this way either. A society that destroys the
family destroys itself.

In the Anglican Catechism quoted earlier on, we see the
word "succour" – this means to run to help. We are to run
to help our parents. The Lutheran Catechism states: "If my
father and mother have any defect I am required to bear it
patiently." Today we have the option of Old People's
Homes. Maybe this is the only way they can really be cared
for. But it is certainly true to say that some of the elderly do
not want to be there and would not need to be there if their
children would care for them. No doubt there are occasions
when a nursing home is absolutely essential but we feel that
we cannot support them financially. Jesus said some people
pretend that to be the case because they have put their
money in a particular investment, leaving them no money
to assist their parents (Mark 7:8–13).

Jesus left us with a moving example – even while He was
hanging on a cross under the burden of the sin of mankind,
in physical agony. In those last moments He remembered
His elderly mother for whom He had a responsibility to
care and said to His mother, " 'Dear woman, here is your
son' and to His disciple (John), 'Here is your mother.'

From that time on this disciple took her into his home"
(John 19:26–27).

"Honour" – it covers the good relationship we should
have with our parents from the day we are toddlers to the
day when our parents die – and in memory of them beyond
that!

6

You shall not murder.

(Exodus 20:13)

On the one hand . . .

Medical science does its utmost to uphold and preserve life. Death is seen as a failure so we strive to prevent it. Heroic and difficult operations are performed in an attempt to maintain life. People often say that medicine has made the life of man longer. This is partly true – but it is not the whole truth. The Biblical estimate for man's lifetime is three score years and ten which is seventy (Psalm 90:10). This was written well before the advent of modern medicine, yet it contains an estimate that remains true today. Modern medicine has not increased man's maximum life-span. What it has done is to enable more people to achieve the maximum possible. The oft-quoted miracles of modern medicine, from vaccination to organ transplants, have had a dramatic effect on the life-span of the average man – an effect for which we are all grateful – but they have done nothing to stretch the maximum!

Life is highly prized and we are appalled when it is lost, particularly in the case of somebody young.

On the other hand

We are hardened to the deaths of our fellow-men and regard them as inevitable. Thousands die each day through starvation and war. Some people feel proud that our latest weapons which are computer controlled are so sophisticated that we cannot miss. It has been said that life was cheap in the past, but surely it is cheaper today when you can kill without seeing the blood.

"War is an extension of foreign policy" (Karl von Clausewitz, Prussian military theorist, 1780–1831). What a terribly inadequate definition of war! Some wars have been brief. Others have dragged on for decades. Death in war is terrible. No animal species can begin to compete with man in the way in which he slaughters his own kind in war.

Death in war is both the most public and the most anonymous of deaths. War is given great attention by the mass media and by the Government. Who are the legions of the dead? The tombs of the "Unknown Soldiers" and the endless war cemeteries throughout the world filled with identical gravestones cry out against the faceless fate of death in battle.

In this century some 9,700,000 people perished in World War I and the toll of World War II was probably around 55,000,000. In 1939, nearly 9,000,000 Jews were living in 20 European States soon to be over-run by Nazi Germany. By 1945, almost 6,000,000 of those 9,000,000 Jews had perished in a planned programme of annihilation. The reason lay in the ideology of the totalitarian Nazi Party which ruled Germany between 1933 and 1945. The Nazis declared that all these people were "racially degenerate" and therefore expendable – fit only for providing slaves for a more superior "Aryan race" as represented by their German conquerors. Massacre does not just happen in world wars either. It is estimated that over 25 million people have died in war *since* World War II.

Advances in technology are largely responsible for the increases in death noted above. Of course it is not just direct hostile action that is responsible for the deaths of civilians during wartime. There are indirect deaths from disease, malnutrition and, if their homes are destroyed, from cold.

Life comes from God and belongs to God

God is the author and giver of life. Life is our greatest gift from God. God is the only one who has the power to give life and God is the only one who has the power to take it away. To regard human beings as expendable, as pawns in a game, and to regard the death of other human beings as of little consequence, ignores the intrinsic value of the human being. We are made in the image of God. "Let us make man in our image" (Genesis 1:26), "So God created man in his own image" (Genesis 1:27). Man is special in creation – however much that image is marred by sin, no other creature reflects the Creator in the way that man does.

Because life comes from God and belongs to God, we must respect our own lives and the lives of others. We are stewards of life. A steward is one who takes care of something for someone else. In the case of life, we should watch over all that God has given us – body, soul, spirit – and over other people too. Our judgements about life should always be made in the light of how we are caring for the great gift that God has given us. Dr Albert Schweitzer commented that there should be "reverence for life".

What this commandment is not about

1. *It is not about the killing of animals*

There is no basis from this commandment or from the rest of the Bible for arguing against the slaying of animals. The misunderstanding has arisen over the translation of the word "rasah" which means "murder", but has on occasions been translated "kill". Failure to understand that has led some to cite Biblical authority against all forms of killing.

2. *It is not about accidental killing*

"This is the rule concerning the man who kills another and flees there to save his life – one who kills his neighbour unintentionally, without malice aforethought. For instance, a man may go into the forest with his neighbour to cut wood and as he swings his axe to fell a tree, the head may fly off and hit his neighbour and kill him. That man may flee to one of these cities and save his life. Otherwise, the avenger of blood might pursue him in a rage . . . and kill him even though he is not deserving of death" (Deuteronomy 19:4–6).

Although a man in the Old Testament could not be put to death for accidental killing, as Deuteronomy shows, he could be put to death for carelessness and negligence in taking life: "When you build a new house, make a parapet around your roof so that you may not bring the guilt of bloodshed on your house if someone falls from the roof" (Deuteronomy 22:8).

Considerable thought is put into the prevention of death by misadventure, but accidental death is still very much a part of our lives. There must be some degree of contributory negligence, which can range from the absence of an adequate warning system to the failure to heed one which does exist. The poet, Steve Turner, made a shrewd comment: "History repeats itself – has to, no-one listens."

In Jesus' day and for many years before that, murder had been defined by the religious leaders as merely the external act. But God looks on the heart and is therefore concerned with attitudes also. Jesus said: "You have heard that it was said to the people long ago, 'Do not murder and anyone who murders will be subject to judgement.' But I tell you that anyone who is angry with his brother will be subject to judgement" (Matthew 5:21–22). Of course there is right-eous anger. But our anger is not often righteous! We harbour grudges, gossip and slander and if "Looks could kill" – who would be standing?

3. *It is not about capital punishment*

Capital punishment was prescribed by God for the people of the Old Testament times for certain offences – of which murder was one. "If anyone takes the life of a human being, he must be put to death" (Leviticus 24:17). "Anyone who kills a person is to be put to death as a murderer only on the testimony of witnesses. But no-one is to be put to death on the testimony of only one witness" (Numbers 35:30).

However, the Old Testament ruling of: "life for life, eye for eye, tooth for tooth, hand for hand, foot for foot" (Deuteronomy 19:21) was a limiting law. It was actually preventing excessive punishment.

Jesus of course instructed His followers to, "Love your enemies, do good to those who hate you, bless those who curse you, pray for those who ill-treat you. If someone strikes you on one cheek, turn to him the other also" (Luke 6:27–29). The Apostle Paul underlines Jesus' teaching. "Do not repay anyone evil for evil. Be careful to do what is right in the eyes of everybody. If it is possible, as far as it

depends on you, live at peace with everyone" (Romans 12:
17–18).

The issue at stake here is this. Could we, in the light of
Jesus' teaching, act as an executioner for a convicted
murderer? If we cannot say yes, then we should not expect
anyone else to do it either. Read John 8:3–11.

4. *It is not about pacifism*

As always, we must take the general tenor of the Bible's
teaching – not isolated sayings – in trying to establish what it
says about pacifism. We must be careful about how we
interpret individual sayings. John the Baptist did not tell
the soldiers who asked what they should do to change their
occupation (Luke 3:14).

Jesus used a whip of cords to clear the Temple court
(John 2:15). This may show His readiness to use physical
force in certain circumstances – but no evidence "to kill".
In warning His disciples of danger ahead, He used the
words "sell your cloak and buy a sword" (Luke 22:36).
When the disciples said in reply: "See, Lord, here are two
swords" (Luke 22:38), Jesus replied, "That is enough",
which could be interpreted as, "Enough of that, you have
misunderstood me." In teaching about the future Jesus
spoke of "wars and rumours of wars" as occurring before
the end (Mark 13:7). Jesus' statement, "I did not come to
bring peace, but a sword" (Matthew 10:34), does not mean
that it was His mission to stir up trouble. He is merely
stating what will unfortunately be one result of His mission.

If I see a child being molested, I have an obligation to
protect the child. I cannot just stand by while evil and
injustice are being carried out. In other words, I am obliged
to protect others. The phrase "just war" has been adopted
to explain when Christians can be involved in war. A
Christian may be involved in a just war providing there is no

other way of maintaining justice and the rights of human beings. But Jesus said: "For all who draw the sword will die by the sword" (Matthew 26:52). Jesus says that when men and women take the law into their own hands and try to establish their point of view by force, they will themselves (at some time) perish by the sword. Jesus' words in Matthew 26 verse 52 are not a command to refrain from fighting, but a reminder of a well-known, though often forgotten, truth.

We should not take the law into our own hands. Where an injustice is to be dealt with, it should be done through the medium of the community. A State has an obligation to use a certain amount of force to ensure that its citizens are permitted to live in peace and safety and if the state fails to do that, it ensures that evil will prosper in an imperfect world.

Of course, we have now got to the stage where any further world war would involve the loss of millions of lives. We are therefore faced with a serious question: even if we do believe in a "just war", is justice and freedom worth more than millions and millions of human lives? I personally doubt it.

What about abortion?

This is relevant to both women and *men*. Many men think that it is only up to women to think this one through – they are wrong! Researchers find it difficult, actually impossible, to say when a developing baby (they would use the words foetus or embryo) becomes capable of existing on its own. The logical approach is to go back to the sperm and the egg. A sperm has 23 chromosomes. An egg also has 23 chromosomes. Once there is the union of sperm and egg they become one cell with 46 chromosomes. That one cell will, if not interrupted, make a human being just like you with the potential for God-consciousness – just like you. Would anyone kill a newborn baby the minute it was born? What about five minutes before, or five minutes before that, or five minutes before that, and so on? At what time can a life be considered worthless, when the next minute that same life has worth?

David wrote:

> You created my inmost being;
> you knit me together in my mother's womb.
> I praise you because I am fearfully and wonderfully
>   made;
> your works are wonderful.
> I know that full well.
> My frame was not hidden from you
> when I was made in the secret place.
> When I was woven together in the depths of the earth,
> your eyes saw my unformed body.
> All the days ordained for me
> were written in your book
> before one of them came to be.

(Psalm 139:13–16)

The author of the Psalm looks back to the ante-natal stage of his existence. Three words sum up what he believes. First, *creation*. He seems to compare God to a weaver who created his inmost being: "you knit me together in my mother's womb" (verse 13). Although the Bible makes no claim to be a textbook of embryology, here is a plain affirmation that the growth of the foetus is neither haphazard nor automatic – but a divine work of creative skill.

The second word is *continuity*. The writer surveys his life in four stages: past (verse 1), present (verses 2–6), future (verses 7–12) and before birth (verses 13–16); and in all

four he refers to himself as "I". He who is writing as an
adult has the same personal identity as the foetus in his
mother's womb. He affirms a direct continuity between his
ante-natal and post-natal being.

The third word is *communion*. Psalm 139 is a statement
of God's personal relationship to the individual. God
knows us intimately (verses 1–6) and attaches himself to us
so that we cannot escape from him (verses 7–12). He
formed us in the womb and established His relationship
with us at that time (verses 13–16). When God called
Jeremiah to be a prophet, He said this:

> Before I formed you in the womb I knew you,
> before you were born I set you apart.
> (Jeremiah 1:5)

Other translations put: "before you came to birth I conse-
crated you", and: "before you came to birth I sanctified
you". This insight is also supported by the New Testament
statement that God knew us from before the foundation of
the world.

The foetus is not a growth in the mother's body, nor even
a potential human being. The foetus is a human life who,
though not yet mature, has the potential to grow into the
fullness of the humanity he already has.

The rest of the Bible endorses this perspective. An
expectant mother is described as "a woman with child".
When the pregnant Elizabeth, carrying John the Baptist,
was visited by the pregnant Mary, carrying Jesus, and heard
her greeting, "the baby leaped in her womb for joy" (Luke
1:44).

If the life of the foetus is a human life, we have to think of
mother and unborn child as two human beings at different
stages of maturity. Doctors have to consider that they have
two patients, not one, and seek the well-being of both.

Development before birth

By the time a baby is 18 days old – which is long before the mother is sure that she is pregnant – the heart is already beating. At 45 days you can pick up (electroencephalographic) waves from the baby's developing brain. At eight weeks the fingerprints on the hands have been formed and, except for size, will never change. By 12 weeks he has fingernails, he sucks his thumb and he can recoil from pain. By the fourth month the baby is eight to ten inches in height. In the fifth month, there is a time of lengthening and strengthening – skin, hair and nails grow. This is the month in which the movements of the baby are felt by the mother. In the sixth month, the baby responds to light and sound. He awakes and sleeps, he can hear the beat of his mother's heart and gets hiccups! In the seventh month, the nervous system becomes much more complex, the baby is 16 inches long and weighs about three pounds. In the final two months there is a time of fattening and continued growth.

What is abortion?

Collins English Dictionary defines "abortion" as "an operation or other procedure to terminate pregnancy before the foetus is viable". "Viable" in this case is defined as "having reached a stage of development at which further development can occur independently of the mother". There are four methods of abortion commonly used.

Dilatation and Curettage (D + C)

The cervix is stretched to enable the insertion of medical instruments. The surgeon then scrapes the wall of the uterus, cutting the baby's body to pieces and scraping the placenta from its attachments on the uterine wall.

Suction Abortion

The principle is the same as D + C. A powerful suction tube is inserted through the open cervix. This tears apart the body of the developing baby and his placenta, sucking them into a jar.

Salt Poisoning Abortion

This method is carried out after sixteen weeks of pregnancy. A long needle is inserted through the mother's abdomen, directly into the sac surrounding the baby, and a solution of concentrated salt is injected into it. The baby breathes in and swallows the salt and is poisoned by it. The outer layer of skin is burned off by the high concentration of the salt. It takes one hour for the baby to die. The mother usually goes into labour about a day later and a shrivelled, dead baby is delivered.

Hysterotomy Abortion

This is exactly the same as a Caesarean section with the one difference. In a Caesarean section, the operation is being done to save the life of the baby, whereas in the hysterotomy, the operation is being done to kill the baby. A hysterotomy abortion is used after eighteen weeks. An incision is made in the lower abdomen and through into the uterus so that the baby can be drawn out through the incision. As this requires surgery, the patient is kept in hospital longer – at least until the stitches, or sutures, have been removed.

Exceptions

I personally believe that abortion is allowable on two accounts. First, to prevent or stop pregnancy following a rape. Rather than waiting to see if one is pregnant in a case of rape, one should go as soon as possible – preferably within 14 days of the horrifying experience – to have a D + C.

Secondly, abortion is permissible when a mother's life will be lost if the abortion does not take place. It is worth stressing, however, that with all our modern medical technology such cases are extremely rare.

What about euthanasia?

The literal meaning of the word "euthanasia" is "dying well". So in its strict sense, euthanasia could encompass any medical practice designed to help people die in dignity and peace. However, euthanasia has come to bear the more restricted sense of the intentional killing by a doctor of a patient under certain specified conditions. The most important of these conditions is of course the patient's free consent.

Those who favour "voluntary euthanasia" believe that in a significant number of cases the only way to ensure a peaceful and dignified death is for a doctor to take positive steps to end the patient's life. As English law now stands, this constitutes murder.

It is important to distinguish enthanasia from two practices with which it is sometimes confused. The first is that of allowing a patient who is suffering from a fatal illness to die in peace without being subjected to troublesome treatments which cannot restore him to health or significantly improve his condition. The second is the use of pain-killing drugs to control severe pain – even at the risk of shortening life. These are now generally accepted by the medical profession and raise no problems of moral principle. They are sometimes called "passive" or "indirect" euthanasia.

However, this language is misleading because it obscures important moral distinctions.

The debate about euthanasia involves three issues:

1. The first is one of fact. Are there a significant number of cases in which the only effective way to control pain is to end the patient's life?

2. The second is moral. Are there circumstances in which it is morally permissible for a doctor intentionally to take life?

3. The third concerns the role of legislation. Would it be wise to change the law so as to permit voluntary euthanasia?

As to the question of fact, those who oppose euthanasia claim that with improvements in drugs there are now very few cases in which severe pain cannot be adequately controlled. They claim that the growth of the hospice movement is evidence of this. Supporters of euthanasia contest this claim and challenge the basis for making it. They claim that it is not for doctors but for the individual to decide when life is no longer tolerable.

The moral case in support of euthanasia tends to take two different forms. The first puts the emphasis upon compassion. The appeal to compassion is directed to doctors and others who are in a position to make decisions about those who are terminally ill. The problem is regarded as one of medical ethics. What should doctors do and what should they be allowed by law to do in the case of patients suffering from a disease which is incurable, fatal and painful? Compassion, it is argued, requires that, given the consent of the patient, the doctor should be ready and able to end the patient's life.

The other moral case appeals to a "right to die" on the part of the patient. It is argued that people should be able to sign in advance a request for euthanasia. If the person ever suffered from a serious physical illness that caused him severe distress or rendered him incapable of rational existence, the decision would have been made in advance. The decision would be the patient's and the doctor would be acting as his agent. According to this view, the individual has the moral right – and should be given the legal right – to decide whether, in certain circumstances, he will live or die. He should also be given the right to be medically assisted if he chooses to die.

The moral case against euthanasia concentrates attention upon the role of the doctor who, whether out of compassion or in pursuance of the patient's "right to die", would be called upon to kill the patient or assist in his suicide.

Christianity and most of those in the medical profession are deeply committed to the sanctity of life. Although it is possible to conceive of exceptions in certain extreme situations, we ought to be very reluctant to sanction any departure from it.

The recognition of an individual's "right to die" would take too little account of the ties that bind people to one another and would encourage the sick, the elderly, and the helpless to regard themselves as dispensable.

The legal questions cannot be separated from the moral one. Whether the law should be changed depends on whether changing it would remove greater evils than it would cause.

However carefully a law was drafted, in practice it would be impossible to avoid abuse or to draw the line clearly between cases which the law considered justified and those which it did not.

As Christians, we should heed our God who says:

I put to death and I bring to life.

(Deuteronomy 32:39)

7

You shall not commit adultery.

(Exodus 20:14)

The world's view of adultery

Of all the behaviour that can attack a marriage, adultery is the one recognised as the most serious.

Adultery is voluntary sexual intercourse between a married man or woman with a partner other than the legal spouse. Statistics for extra-marital sexual activity are hard to establish, but it is suggested that by the age of 40 some 25 per cent of wives and 50 per cent of men have committed adultery. These figures given by sociologist Kinsey are probably on the low side.

It is very clear that the last twenty years have seen an unprecedented increase in divorce. In the United Kingdom in 1987, a total of 165,000 divorces were granted. The British divorce rate had increased by 60 per cent in the last 25 years – it is now one of the highest rates in the western world. In the United Kingdom, one in every three marriages break up; in the States it is more than one in every two. When we compare the number involved in any other social problem, including unemployment, then marital breakdown clearly emerges as one of the most important social upheavals of our age. Currently one in three marriages end in divorce.

Adultery can vary from the casual fling to the deep, personal involvement where an affair becomes a permanent relationship. The intense, long drawn out triangle of which films, magazines and novels are made is glamorised but, in real life, it is exceedingly painful and stressful. We have even got to the stage of a more legalised form of adultery where you get a quick-and-easy divorce – Hollywood style – in preparation for remarriage.

Some people numb their consciences. Others find it all a great amusement and even proudly brag about their latest affair or conquest. Others continue in an adulterous relationship simply out of apathy, convenience or fear of offending their lovers and possible ramifications if the private relationship became public knowledge. Others are locked in an unhappy marriage, seeking solace elsewhere because they see no hope of things improving at home. The film *Fatal Attraction* portrayed the consequences of adultery.

The Bible's view of adultery

What does the Bible teach on adultery? It clearly and simply forbids it. "You shall not commit adultery." In the Old Testament, adultery was considered such a serious sin that it was punished by death. "If a man commits adultery with another man's wife . . . both the adulterer and the adulteress must be put to death" (Leviticus 20:10). Proverbs 6 tells us in verse 32, "a man who commits adultery lacks judgement; whoever does so destroys himself". When a nation lowers its sexual standards of behaviour, then those people have built into themselves the seeds of their own destruction.

Why did God say "No" to adultery? Adultery is a sin against marriage. The Bible has a very high view of marriage. Whenever Jesus was questioned about marriage, divorce or adultery, He always went back to the accounts of

creation to remind His listeners of the perfect standard that
God laid down when He breathed life into man and
woman. For example, in Matthew 19, Jesus is in debate
with some Pharisees about divorce.

> 'Is it lawful for a man to divorce his wife for any and every
> reason?' 'Haven't you read,' he replied, 'that at the
> beginning the Creator "made them male and female",
> and said, "For this reason a man will leave his father and
> mother and be united to his wife, and the two will become
> one flesh"? So they are no longer two, but one. There-
> fore what God has joined together, let man not
> separate.'
>
> (Matthew 19:3–6)

Jesus is quoting Genesis 2:24 (KJV), "Therefore shall a
man leave his father and his mother and shall cleave unto
his wife, and they shall be one flesh."

This statement is repeated four times in the Bible
(Malachi 2:15; Matthew 19:5; Mark 10:7; Ephesians 5:31).
In Matthew's and Mark's Gospels, it is completed with:
"Therefore what God has joined together, let man not
separate" (Matthew 19:6; Mark 10:9). So Jesus makes
three clear statements about marriage: leaving, cleaving
and one flesh.

What constitutes a marriage in God's sight

This is the eternal triangle – not the husband, wife and the
other woman – but the three factors that make a solid
foundation for marriage: leave, cleave, one flesh. Marriage
corresponds to these three things: the legal, social responsibility – leave; the personal, emotional commitment –

cleave; the physical union – one flesh. These three aspects constitute a marriage in God's sight. The reason adultery is so serious is because it breaks into the unity that two people have in marriage.

Leave

"A man will leave his mother and father" was said in the garden of Eden. This is rather interesting because Adam and Eve had no parents. But right at the start, the Lord God makes an important statement. God recognises that in marriage other people will be involved. As we all know, when a marriage takes place, people other than the couple are very much involved. There are relationships in-law as well as in-love.

In marriage, leaving involves a couple breaking the basic unit of society – the family. The new couple leave their parents and they break the old family unit. So you leave one family unit and build a new one. There is a legal, social responsibility in marriage.

Cleave

"Therefore shall a man . . . cleave to his wife." This means to hold together. The original Hebrew word actually means to glue. So a man leaves Mum and Dad to be glued to his wife. It is a good picture which has very clear implications. If you glue two pieces of paper together and later try to tear them apart, you do not tear the glue, you tear the paper. That is exactly what happens in the separation – people are torn.

In the marriage service, vows are made in the name of God:

> I, John, take you Killy,
> to be my wife
> to have and to hold
> from this day forward.
> For better, for worse,
> for richer, for poorer,
> in sickness and in health
> to love and to cherish
> till death us do part,
> according to God's Holy Law
> and this is my solemn vow

In the marriage service, we do not promise to maintain romantic love and erotic love, we promise "to love and to cherish till death us do part". This love is not something of the head or the heart but of the will. That is why we are asked: "Will you promise?" We cannot promise with romantic or erotic love. However, we can promise with the love talked about here because it is modelled on God's love for us and God's love for us is based on His will towards us. It is something He decides. Love is a voluntary, conscious, deliberate decision to stay together "for richer or poorer, in sickness and in health . . . till death us do part". It is a decision and a promise that is made and therefore can be kept.

In English we use the word "love" to mean so many things that we never know for sure what we are talking about. The early Greeks encountered this problem and so they created four different words for love.

The first word is "Philia" which means "brotherly love". Philia is friendship, companionship, the emotional sharing of time and interests. It shows a desire to co-operate.

The second word is "storge". Storge means affection, good-will, concern, kindness. This is the kind of love most often shown by the world to the elderly, to children and neighbours, sincere love but not necessarily deep.

The third word is "eros". It is the root of the word erotic. Eros also means sexual attraction with the act of sex. H. Norman Wright in his book *Pillars of Marriages* defines eros as "love that seeks sensual expression". It is a desire inspired by the biology within us.

Fourthly, the word "Agape" which is what the marriage service is talking about. Agape means a love which comes from realising and understanding the value and precious-ness of a person. It is the "God" kind of love. He realises and understands how precious you are. The character and quality of this love is determined by the character of God. Agape means "selflessness", agape means total giving love. This is the love God expressed when He *gave* His only Son. He had no self-interest. In the human sphere, agape love is thoughtfulness, concern and sensitivity to the needs of others.

Referring to agape love in marriage, the Apostle Paul, in Ephesians 5:28–29, wrote: "In this same way, husbands ought to love (agape) their wives as their own bodies. He who loves his wife loves himself. After all, no-one ever hated his own body, but he feeds it and cares for it, just as Christ does the Church."

You spell this love G-I-V-E. In a giving relationship there is no room for fear, frustration, pressure, envy or jealousy. And thank God that it is the kind of love He has for me and you. The only security I have that God my Father will not fall out of love with me is that He never "fell in love with me". God does not look down and say, "Oh, J. John . . . my heart has just missed a beat." God says, "I agape you." It is that kind of love that holds a marriage together.

You often hear prospective divorcees say "I don't love her any more." Is it "don't" or "won't"? It is not you "can't" but "won't". God says you *can* wilfully agape. And that is why God said, "I hate divorce" (Malachi 2:16). It is anti-agape love and anti-God.

In Jesus' day there were two schools of thought. A strict school of teaching led by the Rabbi Shami who stated that divorce was only permissible on the grounds of adultery. The other school led by Rabbi Hillel who stated that divorce was allowable if you found some indecency in your wife. In Jesus' day "some indecency" could have meant she burnt your dinner, spoke too loudly in the street or talked to another man. Provided you found some indecency in her, all you had to do to divorce her was to hand her a certificate in front of two witnesses.

You can guess which Rabbi had the largest congregation! So by the time Jesus was teaching, marriage had become very cheap. In the passage we started with at the beginning of this chapter (Matthew 19), the Pharisees came to Jesus and asked Him which line He took. Jesus stepped right over to Shami's side and said: "I tell you that anyone who divorces his wife, except for marital unfaithfulness, and marries another woman commits adultery" (Matthew 19:9).

The New Testament allows divorce for only two reasons. The first is adultery, as we have just seen. If one partner breaks the flesh relationship, the other *may* divorce. It does not say the other must. Before resorting to divorce, the first thing is to try forgiveness.

The only other reason for divorce is spiritual incompatibility, when one partner is a Christian and the other is not. However, it is the unbeliever who must take the initiative in that situation.

If any brother has a wife who is not a believer and she is willing to live with him, he must not divorce her. And if a woman has a husband who is not a believer and he is willing to live with her, she must not divorce him. For the unbelieving husband has been sanctified through his wife, and the unbelieving wife has been sanctified through her believing husband. Otherwise your children would be unclean, but as it is, they are holy. But if the unbeliever leaves, let him do so. A believing man or woman is not bound in such circumstances; God has called us to live in peace. How do you know, wife, whether you will save your husband? Or, how do you know, husband, whether you will save your wife?

(1 Corinthians 7:12–16)

That narrows the Christian down to only one situation in which he can take the initiative.

One flesh

When both the social, legal responsibility and the personal commitment are established then follows physical union. That is God's unchanging order for marriage. It was ordained this way before mankind fell into sin.

To say that sex equals sin is nonsense. It is equally wrong to say that sex equals love and to talk about sex as making love. Sex does not make love. Love makes sex. That is God's teaching. Sex is the expression of love and a wonderful reinforcement of it. Within the framework of legal, social responsibility and personal commitment, sex reinforces the relationship. Outside those two things it becomes destructive.

The physical union used to be called the "consummation of marriage". The meaning behind "consummation" is "to put the finishing touch to something". Physical union or sexual intercourse puts the finishing touch to accepted legal social responsibility and emotional personal commitment. It basically crowns it all! This involves the whole of me. It is a physical act in which you give your all. Two become one flesh. That is how powerful it is and it is because of this that adultery is serious – because adultery is a sin against the body.

The Apostle Paul was a Jew – as Jesus was. They lived in Jewish communities and breathed in the Jewish religious and ethical atmosphere. Unmarrieds were supposed to be virgins. A man who slept with a woman outside of marriage could be punished severely, either in a financial way or by death, depending on the circumstances. This, as we have seen, continued into marital life – adultery could be punished by death.

However, sexual ideals in the Roman world, and especially in Greece, were not the same. Alfred Edersheim, a nineteenth-century theologian, commented that "it would be safe to say that chastity was nowhere esteemed in the Hellenistic world except among the Jews".

To the Greeks the body was unimportant. The body was basically a tomb and because of this attitude it did not matter what you did with the body. Premarital and extra-marital sex was therefore judged to be a minor failing – if a fault at all. Homosexuality, incest and other sexual deviations were not uncommon and often the law ignored them.

Christians coming to first-century Corinth found that sexual standards were low. Corinth, a commercial city, was notorious as a hotbed of every kind of vice. "To live like a Corinthian" meant complete moral collapse. A "Corinthian girl" and a "prostitute" were synonymous.

When the Apostle Paul wrote to the Romans he was at that time in Corinth and could write easily as illustrations abounded:

Even their women exchanged natural relations for un-natural ones. In the same way the men also abandoned natural relations with women and were inflamed with lust for one another. Men committed indecent acts with other men, and received in themselves the due penalty for their perversion . . . Although they know God's righteous decree that those who do such things deserve death, they not only continue to do these very things but also approve of those who practise them.

(Romans 1:26–27,32)

Corinth had become a by-word in Paul's day for immorality, rather like Amsterdam today. The Apostle had to be extremely straight and serious. "Do you not know that the wicked will not inherit the Kingdom of God? Do not be deceived. Neither the sexually immoral nor idolaters nor adulterers, nor male prostitutes nor homosexual offenders nor thieves nor the greedy nor drunkards nor slanderers nor swindlers will inherit the Kingdom of God" (1 Corinthians 6:9–10).

He says that this way of living causes serious violations of the Christian way of life. In fact, these were so serious that those who practised them were excluded from membership in the church – and, ultimately, of course, from eternal life with God. We cannot be Christ's followers and conduct ourselves along these lines.

In defining his position and emphasising the wrongness of fornication (pre-marital sex) and adultery, the Apostle Paul shows great understanding of sexual relations.

The body is not meant for sexual immorality, but for the Lord, and the Lord for the body . . . Do you not know that your bodies are members of Christ Himself? Shall I then take the members of Christ and unite them with a prostitute? Never! Do you not know that he who unites himself with a prostitute is one with her in body? For it is said, 'The two will become one flesh' . . . Flee from sexual immorality. All other sins a man commits are outside his body, but he who sins sexually sins against his own body. Do you not know that your body is a temple of the Holy Spirit who is in you, whom you have received from God? You are not your own, you were bought at a price. Therefore honour God with your body.

(1 Corinthians 6:13–20)

The Apostle is saying that sexual relations cannot remain a merely casual affair. A oneness exists so close that it produces an identity of flesh. Such a union flows over into the whole being of the persons involved and cannot be limited just to a surface entanglement soon to be forgotten. Psychologists confirm this. Then the Apostle moves on to a spiritual level and reminds us that through faith and baptism we became intimately united with Jesus, our Saviour, Lord and God.

In a nutshell

The essence of marriage is this – to promise, to make a vow, to offer one's heart and body to the beloved for life. There is a commitment made here before God and family and friends to live and give in sickness and in health. It is not just a piece of paper because God's life is present in and vital to the husband/wife relationship. It is a sacrament. The sacrament of marriage is not just a ceremony that says "now you can make love with the church's blessing". A sacrament is an event, a happening, in which God touches our lives in a special way with the power to help us become – as we "will" – what we are meant to be. The ceremony of marriage tells the world that this man and woman now publicly before their Maker and their fellow men vow to share each other's lives together. Only death will cut the cord which now joins them.

The husband and wife who so seal hearts and hopes together at the altar join their bodies together in the marriage bed. Sexual intercourse deepens their commitment to each other, it physically expresses their total union. Adultery kills.

How do we respond to this?

This is a challenge to the church and especially church leaders. We have an obligation to discipline.

> If your brother sins against you, go and show him his fault, just between the two of you. If he listens to you, you have won your brother over. But if he will not listen, take one or two others along, so that 'every matter may be established by the testimony of two or three witnesses'. If he refuses to listen to them, tell it to the church; and if he refuses to listen even to the church, treat him as you would a pagan or a tax collector.
>
> (Matthew 18:15–17)

We have an obligation to confront people *privately* about their sin. We need to go to them and be honest. Sin is not a social inconvenience which we just sweep under the carpet.

To the single readers

You are probably feeling, if you have read this chapter, that this commandment is rather academic because you are not married. However, we live in a sex-permeated society in which there is a lot of talk about pre-marital sex (fornication).

There are some ridiculous ideas that have been circulating around for years. One of them is that faithful married couples have sex just out of routine and that only the so-called swingers really tap the full potential of sex. Listen here, that is stupid! If God knows what is best for us – and He does – and His laws are intended to guide us towards real happiness, then the results will show that, won't they? And they do. I do not know anyone, and I've talked to quite a few people, who waited for sex until their marriage and then felt they had been silly and cheated from all the excitement they could have had while the opportunities were going. Sex is part of the eros love God designed. Sex when practised in love and in the confines of marriage is holy and pure. "Marriage should be honoured by all, and the marriage bed kept pure, for God will judge the adulterer and all the sexually immoral" (Hebrews 13:4).

The word virginity has almost fallen out of use. Peer pressure, false or unbridled emotions, plus lack of appreciation as to its seriousness and possible consequences, have led to a great deal of pre-marital sex experimentation. The modern argument is, "Those who have experienced intimate sexual relationships before marriage will be better sex partners in marriage." But if you love someone enough to marry them, you are really not going to be embarrassed at lack of "experience". God created us male and female and sex was designed only to be in the confines of marriage.

Keep yourself for the person you are going to marry. Do not date unbelievers because their standards are different from yours. Read 2 Corinthians 6:14–16. It is almost certain they will expect you to sleep with them. Some say, "but we love each other". Will that love last? If you do have sexual intercourse but later break up and go your separate ways, what do you tell the next partner? Couples in love at moments of tenderness and intimacy feel this relationship will never break up. Can they be certain before they vow "until death do us part"?

Keep yourself for the person you are going to marry. Fornication is a sin against the marriage you may have in the future. Jesus Christ even said you can commit adultery with your thoughts: "Anyone who looks at a woman lustfully has already committed adultery with her in his heart" (Matthew 5:28). There is a law against rape, but there is no law against looking at pornographic pictures. But Jesus links the two – thought and action. We need to be alert and wise. If situations cause you to sin do not walk into those situations. If your eye causes you to sin, do not look. Get into the habit of guarding the approaches to sin. For example, pornography – like so many other evils – is a situation where beauty has been corrupted. Shakespeare wrote, "Lilies that fester smell far worse than weeds". What Shakespeare is saying (I think) is that if something is beautiful then the more awful and messed up it becomes if it is abused.

"Blessed are the pure in heart, for they will see God" (Matthew 5:8).

To those who have committed adultery or are committing adultery now

Many Christians live lives that are not free from the imprisoning feelings of guilt. Often they believe these feelings are God's way of punishing them. They are sadly mistaken. Feelings of guilt that lead to further negative emotions are not from God. They do not set us free as God intends us to be. The first negative emotion experienced by man was when Adam and Eve felt shame about their nakedness. Shame is a form of guilt. Their feelings of guilt, like ours, were an internal response to sin they had committed. Instead of leading them to repentance, Adam and Eve's guilt led to the negative action of hiding in an attempt to escape God's punishment. Feeling guilty is an internal emotional conflict arising out of something we have done, said or thought which we know is wrong. It may even be that you do not feel guilty. Your habitual sinning over a period of time may have immuned your spiritual system. *You* are in a serious situation. TAKE NOTE!

As Christians we are endeavouring to follow Christ our Lord and we find that sin is a great problem. We all identify with the Apostle Paul's frustrated experience of finding himself doing the evil things he did not want to do: "I do not understand what I do. For what I want to do I do not do, but what I hate I do" (Romans 7:15).

The night before Jesus died, in the Garden of Gethsemane, Jesus looked for support and comfort from his closest friends. They knew and understood this yet they failed him. He asked them to stay awake – yet they fell asleep. Many of us have broken promises, have failed slightly and seriously in honesty, self-control and sex. But some servants of God have not succumbed to these temptations. They are people of courage and that is what is needed. Only strong, determined, courageous people who trust Christ's power to help them, can ever resist the pull of weak human nature and society with its free love pro-sex emphasis.

Our failures can be divided into two groups, temporary mistakes and permanent ones when we refuse to acknowledge God's grace and our responsibility for what we do. With the permanent failures, we give in, with feelings of defeat and depression. We can rebel and keep on sinning. We may even confess our failure, our sin – but without repentance. This is like promising your mother to do some housework just to get her off your back. It is simply a defence to allow us to keep on doing what we want and avoid real change. Basically with permanent mistakes we just give up, fail to learn from them, lock ourselves into self-pity, refuse to forgive ourselves and reject God's forgiveness, mercy, grace and strength to continue.

With the temporary failures, we do learn, we learn not to give up, we forgive ourselves and others and come to the Lord for forgiveness and strength. Our errors may be gigantic, but if we rise above them, then the failure is not permanent.

If you have committed adultery, you are going to have to talk about it with your real partner and ask forgiveness. You and your real partner may need to see a counsellor. This is very delicate and painful, but it needs to be done in the context of self-forgiveness and receiving God's forgiveness.

We must learn from our errors and the factors that contributed to them in order to be on guard and alert in the future. Jesus' words to the woman taken in adultery are helpful here:

[They] said to Jesus, 'Teacher, this woman was caught in the act of committing adultery. In the Law Moses commanded us to stone such women. Now what do you say?' . . . 'If any one of you is without sin, let him be the first to throw a stone at her.'. . . At this, those who heard began to go away one at a time . . . until only Jesus was left, with the woman still standing there. Jesus . . . asked her, 'Woman, where are they? Has no-one condemned you?' 'No-one, sir,' she said. 'Then neither do I condemn you,' Jesus declared. 'Go now and leave your life of sin.'
(John 8:4–11)

Jesus forgave the woman but expected her to learn from her error and not do it again.

Receiving God's forgiveness

We have many accounts of people's failings in the Bible.
One of these is very relevant to our thinking here. There is
an account of David and his failings with Bathsheba (2
Samuel 11 and 12). David the King was anointed by God
and chosen as the leader of the chosen people. He sent his
servants out to battle while he remained in Jerusalem:

> One evening David got up from his bed and walked
> around on the roof of the palace. From the roof he saw a
> woman bathing. The woman was very beautiful, and
> David sent someone to find out about her. The man said,
> 'Isn't this Bathsheba, the daughter of Eliam and the wife
> of Uriah the Hittite?' Then David sent messengers to get
> her. She came to him, and he slept with her . . . Then she
> went back home. The woman conceived and sent word to
> David, saying, 'I am pregnant.'
>
> (2 Samuel 11:2–5)

So David then summoned Uriah, her husband, from the
battle front. He hoped he would sleep with his wife and so
remove any suspicion from the king as the child's father.
But Uriah was such a noble soldier that he felt he could not
go to his home and eat, drink and sleep with his wife while
his fellow comrades were in the middle of a battle. David
then invited Uriah to his palace and gave him food and
drink and "made him drunk". Yet Uriah still did not go to
his wife.

The king then sent Uriah back to the battle front with a
letter for his commander. The letter instructed the commander to place Uriah in the front line, where the fighting
was the hardest and most dangerous so that "he may be
struck down and die". This is exactly what happened.

"When Uriah's wife heard that her husband was dead,

she mourned for him. After the time of mourning was over, David had her brought to his house, and she became his wife and bore him a son. But the thing David had done displeased the Lord" (2 Samuel 11:26-27).

God sent the prophet Nathan to the sinning king. Nathan told David a story about two men – one rich, the other poor. The rich man dealt the poor one a really severe blow, taking the only thing he owned, a small lamb. "David burned with anger against the man and said to Nathan, 'As surely as the Lord lives, the man who did this deserves to die! He must pay for that lamb four times over, because he did such a thing and had no pity'" (2 Samuel 12:5-6).

David did not see the parallel with his own sin. So Nathan drove the point home and said to the king: "You are the man! This is what the Lord, the God of Israel, says, 'I anointed you king over Israel, and I delivered you from the hand of Saul . . . Why did you despise the word of the Lord by doing what is evil in His eyes?'" (2 Samuel 12:7-9). Nathan continued and eventually David admitted, "I have sinned against the Lord." Nathan then spoke to David of God's forgiveness, but added that a continuing punishment would afflict David because of his sin.

"The Lord has taken away your sin. You are not going to die. But because by doing this you have made the enemies of the Lord show utter contempt, the son born to you will die" (2 Samuel 12:13-14).

And so today, we too wander away from God, eventually turn back and look to Him for forgiveness and mercy, but often there is a residue, a consequence. It will probably not be the death of a child as it was with David – but nevertheless, we may be left with anguish of conscience.

The unfaithful husband or wife and the unwed mother may have received God's forgiveness and forgiven themselves, but is it possible to totally forget? Can we erase those moments of misgiving in our past life? God sometimes heals instantly, but often He allows more time to heal wounds and memories.

As Christians we can find comfort in the New Testament. We have seventeen different instances in which Jesus forgave a sinner and showed mercy. In Luke's Gospel, his critics said, "This man welcomes sinners, and eats with them." Jesus said, "I tell you that in the same way there will be more rejoicing in heaven over one sinner who repents than over ninety-nine righteous persons who do not need to repent" (Luke 15:2,7).

Sometimes, unburdening a past error to someone else can make us feel much better and makes it easier to forgive ourselves. I think the Roman Catholic Church is wise in having this as part of its healing ministry. I have a spiritual director, a monk called Father Thomas, whom I see once a month for a day, for sharing, Bible reading and prayer. Over the ten years that I have been seeing him, there have been occasions where my conscious sin was not dealt with just by my endeavouring to receive God's forgiveness and self-forgiveness. Confessing to Father Thomas was quite healing. He listens and advises and prays to bring the healing and forgiveness of Christ.

There is a lovely story in Luke's Gospel chapter seven. We can assume that the woman involved in the story was Mary Magdalene. A religious leader called Simon invited Jesus to have dinner with him. Simon failed to extend to Jesus the courtesies normally offered to distinguished guests. The guest's feet would normally be washed when entering the home, he would be embraced and kissed by the master of the house and his head sprinkled with perfume before he sat down. Guests sat on cushions and in a house like Simon's would be served by servants. Banquets were also semi-public affairs in which interested persons were free to enter, observe what was happening, admire the food and listen to the conversation. One of these people was

Mary, who "stood behind Him (Jesus) at His feet" (Luke 7:38). What was Mary like? She was a sinner. What kind of sinner? Perhaps she was a prostitute. Mary came to the dinner already equipped with "an alabaster jar of perfume" and "she began to wet Jesus' feet with her tears. Then she wiped them with her hair, kissed them and poured perfume on them."

What she did not only puzzled the host, Simon, but upset him and he said, "If this man (Jesus) were a prophet, He would know who is touching Him and what kind of woman she is – that she is a sinner."

As soon as Simon thought this, Jesus said: " 'Simon, I have something to tell you.' And Simon said, 'Tell me, teacher.' 'Two men owed money to a certain money-lender. One owed him five hundred denarii (a denarius was a coin worth about a day's wage), and the other fifty. Neither of them had the money to pay him back, so he cancelled the debts of both. Now which of them will love him more?' "

The answer was obvious.

Simon replied, 'I suppose the one who had the bigger debt cancelled.' 'You have judged correctly,' Jesus said. Then he turned towards the woman and said to Simon, 'Do you see this woman? I came into your house, you did not give me any water for my feet, but she wet my feet with her tears and wiped them with her hair. You did not give me a kiss, but this woman, from the time I entered has not stopped kissing my feet. You did not put oil on my head, but she has poured perfume on my feet. Therefore, I tell you, her many sins have been forgiven – for she loved much.' . . .

Jesus then turned to Mary and said,

'Your sins are forgiven.' The other guests began to say among themselves, 'Who is this who even forgives sins?'

And Jesus continued, applying further forgiving oil upon the repentant woman, 'Your faith has saved you, go in peace.' (Luke, 7:43–7, 48–50)

When we are repentant, God forgives and forgets our sins. My friend Mary Juckes commented that our forgetfulness in human terms is a failing – but God's ability to put sins out of His mind is different. If God really has forgiven us, what purpose would He have in remembering?

Where does one find a "confessor", a "priest-minister"? It can often be quite hard, if you sense you are in this dilemma of "being forgiven and not feeling forgiven", to go to your own minister. If you can, however, then do. Why not now see if you can get a "spiritual-adviser" like I have? Some of us think of monasteries and convents as places of escape, but I believe it is one of their ministries to pray with and for us. Even if you have nothing to confess, you have someone who can listen and advise you.

For me, Father Thomas, my "priest-confessor", represents Christ and his authority. So, after confession, the words "your sins are forgiven you" bring freshness and healing. I leave knowing and feeling that it is all off my chest and believing in my own mind that it has been dealt with. I can trust that this is so because of the Bible and because of Father Thomas, a representative of the Church.

8

> You shall not steal.
>
> (Exodus 20:15)

There must be very few of us who have not broken this commandment. Perhaps when we stole, we did not think of it as stealing or theft — words like take, loot, embezzle, defraud, keep, pinch or make off with might have been used instead. Nonetheless, stealing and theft is what it was.

The view that one should not steal is a generally accepted standard of the human race. There is almost universal condemnation in society for armed robbery, burglary, mugging old ladies for their handbags and many other similar forms of theft. We are angered and appalled by such injustice. It is unacceptable behaviour and we frown upon it. Our reaction of course is right, for these incidents are a violation of God's law and people are harmed in the process. However, our understanding of God's law seems to terminate with the obvious, sometimes violent forms of theft.

What about . . . ?

What about the person who misleads the Income Tax Inspector? An income tax analysis reported the following: "Precise statistics are impossible to obtain since no-one knows the amount of income that escapes taxation through

evasion, unrecorded financial transactions and other similar activities. Inland Revenue officials estimate that the
amount is between £5,000 million and £11,000 million a
year." A staggering sum of money is fiddled each year –
stolen that is!

What about the employee who claims more than is
required for expenses from the company? It is really very
easy to do. For example: a group of four employees have to
go to a meeting and all decide to use one taxi. It would be
simple for each to claim one full taxi fare rather than a
quarter of the taxi fare. Is this not a case of stealing rather
than being clever?

What about when we use the telephone for long personal
conversations rather than for the business we are assigned?
We often hear people say, "Oh it doesn't matter, the firm's
paying." Does the firm know that it is paying? If it does
not know and does not approve, we not only steal but
deceive and lie. I often get personal letters from Christians using company envelopes, by a company franking
machine.

Some will say that this is all legalism because we are only
talking of a few pounds. But the eighth commandment does
not say, "You shall not steal more than £1 at a time." It
says, "You shall not steal."

What about the attitude of trying to get our salary for as
little work as possible – arriving late for work, leaving early,
taking an extended lunch break but calling it a "working
lunch"? Is this stealing or has our employer instructed us to
arrive late, have extended lunch breaks and leave early?
One summer, when I was a student, I got a job with the
County Council in London, cutting grass on road round-
abouts. On the first day, my foreman told me off for
working too fast, "Slow down, otherwise they will expect us
to do the same when you're gone." At the slightest drop of
rain we would sit in a shed. Nearly all my eight weeks with

the County Council was spent reading books, playing cards and taking it easy!

What about the person who charges too much for a product or sells a poor quality product pretending that it is much better than it is? Are we being honest entrepreneurs or thieves?

All these examples have become "respectable theft". Often many of the examples involve a company or the Government, so we find it harder to condemn the culprit. Theft is taking something that belongs to somebody else.

Justifying it by saying "The firm can afford it", or "I don't like what the Government does with our money", in the case of tax evasion, misses the point; it is still stealing and theft.

Why do we steal?

Covetousness

We may steal because of a craving for something which does not belong to us, where we give to a "thing" the loyalty and attention that should be given to God. It is greed and a symptom of insecurity. For some this becomes an obsession – kleptomania, an uncontrollable tendency to steal things with no desire to use or profit by them.

Lack of trust

If we steal then we are demonstrating lack of trust in God the Provider.

The Israelites "forgot what He had done" (Psalm 78:11). The works of God are described in detail – the crossing of the sea; the guidance of the cloud and the pillar of fire; the provision of water, manna and quails. Despite these constant blessings, the people continued to moan and "they

continued to sin against Him" (Psalm 78:17). Has God
failed us? Does God not allow us enough? Despite this
some people steal out of genuine need, not necessarily for
themselves but for their starving children. If we have a need
to steal then we have a lack of trust in God the Provider.

Disobedience

" 'Will a man rob God? Yet you rob me.' But you ask, 'How
do we rob you?' 'In tithes and offerings. You are under a
curse – the whole nation of you – because you are robbing
me' " (Malachi, 3:8–9).

In the Old Testament the Jewish people had to give God
a tenth of all their income to be set aside for the work of
God. However, although they were coming to God in
worship with religious words on their lips, those words were
not supported by action. They were not giving their tithes
and God said, "You are robbing me." Some people today
will say, "I am not a Jew and I am living under grace/under
the New Covenant so I don't have to pay the tithe." But if
the Jews had to pay their tithe under the covenant of law,
how can I give less because I am under the covenant of
grace? Remember that we only give *offerings* to God after
we have given a tenth.

Some people believe that God is very accommodating
and is content when we give 50p every now and then. A
God who is content with less than everything is no God at
all. A God who takes possession of my life takes possession
of all. He teaches me that I am a steward and that I will be
called one day to give an account.

Are we defrauding God of this tithe? We also need to be
careful with our motives and attitudes. We should not pay
our tithes thinking, "Lord, I've been good to you – now you
be good to me." In paying our tithes we act rightly. It is up
to God what He does after that.

Private property

This commandment indirectly establishes the right to private property. The fact that we are not to steal obviously means that what others have rightly belongs to them and is recognised to be theirs by God. The Bible recognises the right for personal property and the Bible does not say "what's his is mine and what's mine is my own". The Bible does not say that ownership and property are wrong and evil. Neither does it condone amassing wealth selfishly without any concern for other people. The Bible's view is that all property is held by its "owner" (or more correctly "guardian" or "steward") as a trust from God Himself. Theft is therefore stealing from God what He has given to another person – removing from a person the trust which God has given them.

This does not mean that God is a capitalist. God is neither a capitalist nor a communist. If you reject all notions of owning property, as anarchists may, then you also reject any sense of personal responsibility for property.

I heard a story about the Anarchist Society which, some years ago at Oxford University, set up a scheme to free bikes from private ownership. They stole bikes and painted them white and said that since they did not belong to anybody, anyone could use them. Any time you saw a white bike, you used it. Most students felt the system worked quite well until the bike got a puncture! Because the bike did not belong to anybody, nobody wanted to mend the puncture. This kind of solution is not the answer and is definitely not Biblical.

A group of early Christians in Jerusalem chose to place their possessions in common ownership following the day of Pentecost (Acts 2:44–45). The case of Ananias and Sapphira has been cited in support of this, for they were struck dead for holding back from the church some of the proceeds from the sale of their property (Acts 5:1–11). Their sin was not that they kept back some of the money, but that they lied to the Holy Spirit and to the members of the church. Such was the white-hot purity of the early church that either they had to go or the Holy Spirit had to go! Neither the Old nor the New Testament forbids private ownership of goods, but the Christian view of stewardship brings responsibility to the way we use our possessions. We who are well provided with this world's goods must make it a priority to use them for the benefit of others.

Now we all like Robin Hood – well, I live in Nottingham and I do. Robin Hood is a hero, robbing the rich to help the poor. However, acting as a Robin Hood is not Biblical. Stealing is out! As Christians, we change society. The rich should take responsibility for how they get their riches and how they use their riches. But let's not worry about them. If I have broken this commandment what should I do?

What must we do?

Repent

"Jesus entered the temple area and drove out all who were buying and selling there. He overturned the tables of the money changers and the benches of those selling doves. 'It is written,' he said to them, 'My house will be called a house of prayer', but you are making it a den of robbers" (Matthew 21:13). Jesus drove them out. However, to the repentant thief on the cross beside Him He said: "today you will be with me in paradise" (Luke 23:43). The thief on the cross knew what he was and he was sorry for it. Jesus received him into His Kingdom.

"Every good and perfect gift is from above, coming down
from the Father" (James 1:17).

To steal is to sin against God and therefore requires
repentance. An example of this is David's Psalm of confession. David stole Bathsheba's good name from her and
even stole her husband's life. Eventually in deep repentance he cried out to God: "Against you, you only, have I
sinned" (Psalm 51:4).

In Luke 15 we have the account of the Prodigal Son who
demanded from his father his inheritance due to him on
his father's death. In other words, his son said, "I want you
to be dead now – give me the money." The father did what
was asked of him. Eventually, having squandered all the
money, the son returned and said, "make me" (Luke
15:19). An amazing contrast between "give me" and
"make me". Let us repent of our sins and ask God our
Father to remake us to honour Him with words and
deeds.

Restoration/Restitution

Zacchaeus was a notorious, despised tax collector who
overcharged people and pocketed the difference. Jesus met
Zacchaeus and Zacchaeus repented (Luke 19) which meant
a completely new direction for his life. The thief on the
cross had no opportunity to put right what he had done
wrong but Zacchaeus had the opportunity and took it.

So Zacchaeus forgets his past, starts a new life and rights
his wrongs: "Zacchaeus stood up and said . . . , 'Look,
Lord! Here and now I give half of my possessions to the
poor, and if I have cheated anybody out of anything, I will
pay back four times the amount.' . . . Jesus said to him,
'Today salvation has come to this house'" (Luke 19:8–9).

The act of restitution (giving back something that has

been stolen) is a strong Biblical theme: "A thief must certainly make restitution" (Exodus 22:3). Theft is an offence against others. It may harm them. It always diminishes them, because it treats them as no longer worthy of our respect or love.

Restore what is not yours to its rightful owner. When I became a Christian in 1975, I was really convicted by many of the things I had stolen. (I hadn't heard a sermon or read Exodus 22:3!) So I innocently gathered about eighteen books, including encyclopaedias that I had stolen from a large bookshop in London, and I took them back. The first sales lady I told nearly fainted. Eventually, I sat in front of the manager and I explained that I had stolen them, but that I had now become a Christian and said I would be quite happy to start paying for them. He was absolutely stunned by my testimony and said that I did not need to pay anything.

Now I am not suggesting we do this with everything we have stolen, but at least ask God what He wants you to do. What about giving your stolen goods to Oxfam! (As we've mentioned books, those of you who have borrowed my books – can I have them back?! I will do likewise!!)

We need to check our honesty and behaviour. We need to be honest in the way we deal with big organisations and the Government. Otherwise, we are hypocrites before God and bad witnesses before men. If we are in the business of influencing the world for Jesus Christ, then we should not allow the world to influence us with the way it carries on. We need to be a consistent witness, glorifying God in every area of our lives. This is going to be hard. We will become unpopular in our place of work. If you send in an expenses claim consistently lower than your colleagues, it is going to be embarrassing both for you and the hierarchy because it challenges an accepted way of life.

Jesus' words are encouraging here. "Whoever lives by

the truth comes into the light, so that it may be seen plainly that what he has done has been done through God" (John 3:21).

Many of us allow ourselves to be deaf to our conscience because of the consequences of following what we believe. The Income Tax Department received an anonymous letter: "I am having trouble sleeping because of my conscience, please find enclosed £100. If this doesn't cure my insomnia I'll send the rest."

Let us fight to hear God's voice through our conscience and to uphold His standards even if it does prove an inconvenience. You will definitely create fuel for conversation about the Christian faith. Always remember the Golden Rule that Jesus gives us: "So in everything, do to others what you would have them do to you, for this sums up the Law and the Prophets" (Matthew 7:12).

9

> You shall not give false testimony against your
> neighbour.
>
> (Exodus 20:16)

Should doctors lie to dying patients in order to delay the
anxiety and fear which the truth might bring them? Should
professors "exaggerate" the excellence of their students in
references in order to give them a better chance in a tight
job market? Should parents conceal from their children the
fact that they were adopted? Should social scientists mas-
querade as patients to doctors in order to learn about racial
and sexual biases in diagnosis and treatment? Should jour-
nalists lie to those from whom they seek information in
order to expose corruption?

Questions of truth and lying pervade all that is said or left
unspoken within our families, our working relationships
and communities. In law and in government, in journalism
and in the social sciences, deception is taken for granted
when it is felt to be excusable by those who tell the lies.
Some government officials, especially those who run for
elections, often deceive when they can get away with it,
particularly if they think that the true state of affairs is
actually beyond comprehension by the general public!
(Being "economical with the truth" is regarded as clever
and shrewd.) In the book *Born Again* by Charles W.
Colson, the former special assistant to USA President
Richard Nixon, we are told of the complete breakdown of
trust between people in the administration. No one knew

who was lying or who was telling the truth. Colson spent seven months in prison for his part in Watergate.

Some lawyers have been known to manipulate the truth in court on behalf of their clients. Sometimes advertisers have misled the public in order to achieve more sales. Psychiatrists may distort information about their patients to preserve confidentiality.

Discovering that we have been lied to in an important personal matter by our family or in a national issue by the government creates disappointment, resentment and suspicion. We feel manipulated. It also makes us wonder in how many other areas we have been deceived. A society whose members are unable to distinguish truthful messages from deceptive ones is bound to collapse: "If like truth, the lie had but one face, we would be on better terms, for we would accept as certain the opposite of what the liar would say. But the reverse of truth has one hundred thousand faces and an infinite field" (Michel de Montaigne, *Essays*).

A lying tongue is included in the infamous list in Proverbs 6:

> There are six things the Lord hates,
> seven that are detestable to Him:
> haughty eyes,
> a lying tongue,
> hands that shed innocent blood,
> a heart that devises wicked schemes,
> feet that are quick to rush into evil,
> a false witness who pours out lies
> and a man who stirs up dissension among brothers.
>
> (Proverbs 6:16–19)

Out of those seven sins that are hated by God, three relate to the tongue, a lying tongue, a false witness and stirring up trouble. Proverbs returns to this subject in chapter 12 verse 22: "Lying lips are an abomination to the Lord" (RSV). The word "abomination" is the strongest word that can be used to describe something that displeases God. This may seem strangely out of proportion, but the context of it is the deep-seated concern for the many people who have suffered from the sins of others.

On top of that: "Outside are the dogs, those who practise magic arts, the sexually immoral, the murderers, the idolaters and everyone who loves and practises falsehood" (Revelation 22:15).

Lies also affect the liar. He knows he is not a man of integrity and he knows, if he is found out, that his credulity and the respect for his word have been damaged. "By a lie a man throws away and, as it were, annihilates his dignity as a man" (Immanuel Kant).

Furthermore, few lies are solitary ones. It is easy to tell a lie – but hard to tell only one. The first lie must be covered up by another. More and more lies are needed. The pressures become greater each time. The liar has to have an excellent memory to keep his untruths disentangled!

Finally, perhaps the most devastating thing about lies is the fact that often they are irretrievable. There is a story of a man who went to see a monk during the Middle Ages. He told the monk that he had sinned because he had been gossiping and telling lies about someone. What should he do? The monk told him to go and put a feather on every doorstep in the town. The man quickly rushed away and did just that. He then came back to the monk. The monk told him to go back and pick up all the feathers. The man said that would be impossible as by now the wind would have blown them all away. The monk told the man that is what had happened with his words!

White lies, right lies?

The simplest rule is to cut out all lies. Many theologians have taken this stand, one of the foremost among them being St Augustine. He wrote that "God forbids *all* lies and that liars therefore endanger their immortal souls." This view was supported by John Wesley, "If any in fact do this, either teach men to do evil that good may come or do so themselves, their damnation is just. This is particularly applicable to those who tell lies in order to do good thereby."

What about white lies? White lies that seem so harmless. The fact that they are so common provides their protective colouring. And their very triviality, when compared to more threatening lies, makes it seem unnecessary or even absurd to condemn them. A white lie is a falsehood not meant to injure anyone. Take for example the many social exchanges, "How nice to see you!"; "Oh, you are looking nice!" These and many other polite greetings and expressions are so much taken for granted that if we decided, in the name of total honesty, not to use them, we would probably give the impression of being cold and indifferent. Should we put on a "face" or be truthful?

We may give a false excuse (lie) so as not to hurt the feelings of someone making an invitation or request and say we "can't" do something when, in reality, we may not "want" to do it. Again, should we be truthful and upset people and begin to break a relationship or give a false excuse? What about at Christmas when one receives a present one does not want, do we lie and say, "That's just what I wanted" or should we be truthful?

Well, we need to be loving and wise with words. There is no need to be blunt and abrasive. Instead of saying "How nice to see you" when you don't mean it, say "Hello". The invitation is a little harder – I would say "unable". As for the Christmas present, be appreciative – you can always give it to Oxfam. I wonder how Augustine and Wesley coped with our everyday examples!

What about the cases where innocent lives are at stake when the costs of lying are small and those of telling the truth catastrophic? Take the example of a ship transporting many Jewish passengers, stopped at a check point by Nazi soldiers who enquire of the Captain whether there are any Jewish passengers on board. If the Captain says the truth the Jews will be shot. If he lies there is a good possibility he is giving them life. To tell the truth is a duty, but it is a duty only toward one who has a right to the truth. I believe it is wise to lie in this situation rather than letting the truth be used for evil purposes. It does not mean the lie is right, but it is the lesser of two evils. Lying is not made right by the circumstances. So if we are going to tell a "white lie" then we must be absolutely sure that is the *only* course we can take in the circumstances – and how often are we in that sort of life and death situation? Usually we tell "white lies" because it is more convenient for us to do so. Our motives are usually self-centred.

Aesop, the Philosopher of the Fables, was once asked what was the most useful thing in the world. "The tongue", he replied. And what was the most harmful thing in the world. "The tongue", he replied once more.

The tongue is the only tool that grows sharper with constant use! The Apostle James writing two thousand years ago said that the tongue, though only a small part of the body, can do enormous damage (James 3:3–5). For two thousand years millions of tongues have proven the truth of that statement.

The tongue causes us more problems than anything else. You only need a spark to start a forest fire, and as we look at the history of the Church, it is obvious that much damage has been done just through the sparks of the tongue.

Gossip, slander and rumours can destroy people. We all know we should not gossip. Yet our thirst for the "news", both hearing and telling it, seems at times insatiable. So we devise ways of sharing it. Can I share something for prayer?! The excuse soothes our consciences. The only time people dislike gossip is when the gossip is about them. If my friend gossips to me about someone else, should I not doubt my friend's loyalty? After all, if he gossips to me, maybe he will gossip about me!

A mother wrote to a women's magazine column asking the counsellor what to do about the rumour (a lie) being spread that her sixteen-year-old daughter was pregnant. The mother wondered if the best thing to do would be to transfer her daughter to another school. The counsellor suggested not, instead let time prove the rumour false. It sounded like good sensible advice. The mother however wrote back months later saying that she did leave her daughter in the same school, and now they are saying that she had an abortion (a lie). What should she do now? The counsellor had no reply. Once false rumours begin they accelerate in destructiveness.

There are many references in the Bible to gossip and slander, among them the following: "Do not go about spreading slander" (Leviticus 19:16). "Gossip is so tasty – how we love to swallow it" (Proverbs 18:8, Good News). Jeremiah's enemies in the Old Testament said: "So come, let's attack him with our tongues and pay no attention to anything he says" (Jeremiah 18:18).

In the New Testament: "If you suffer, it should not be as a murderer or thief or any other kind of criminal, or even as a meddler" (1 Peter 4:15).

It is remarkable that the busybody is listed along with murderers and criminals. Gossip and slander are serious violations of God's will. Why then are they so widespread? It is because we have neutralised ourselves with what we call "good" excuses. However, in the light of examination they are not good excuses but myths.

Myth 1:

"The people I told won't tell anyone else. They promised they wouldn't and we were sharing in confidence." Is this true?

Myth 2:

"I am *just* sharing this so we can pray about it." Is this true? Is prayer our real and only motive?

Myth 3:

"If the information is true then it is fine to share it." Nothing could be further from the truth. The issue is not whether the information is true or false, but whether it is harmful or confidential.

"Do not let any unwholesome talk come out of your mouths, but only what is helpful for building others up according to their needs, that it may benefit those who listen" (Ephesians 4:29).

Why is truth important?

Augustine wrote: "When regard for truth has been broken down or even slightly weakened, all things will remain doubtful."

The reason that truth is so important to God is because truthfulness is part of His nature. Psalm 31:5 tells us that He is a "God of Truth" and in Titus 1:2 we read of God "who does not lie". So our desire and commitment for truth draws us nearer to God and into deeper fellowship with Him. God's word commands us to speak the truth.

Lying against the truth is the strength of Satan's system. Not only does he lie, but he wants us to lie as well and when we lie we support him. That is exactly what Jesus was saying when He said to the Pharisees: "You belong to your father, the devil, and you want to carry out your father's desire. He was a murderer from the beginning, not holding to the truth, for there is no truth in him. When he lies he speaks his native language, for he is a liar and the father of lies" (John 8:44).

Non-truth is the devil's language and the language of the world. So we must be wise and beware. Non-truth is a sin that Satan promotes, whether it be lying to cover up adultery or deceiving to gain some business advantage or bearing false witness. Non-truth supports, promotes and protects the welfare of sin. It is the supporting structure of Satan's system. "Sin has many tools but a lie is the handle that fits them all" (Oliver Wendell Holmes). Samuel Johnson made an interesting observation about the devil: "Yes the devil *is* the father of lies, but he and his colleagues do not lie to one another, since the society of Hell could not subsist without truth any more than others."

Curing the problem

1. *Recognise lying as a problem of the heart and mind*

Jesus talked about the tongue and related it to a tree and its fruit: "Make a tree good and its fruit will be good, or make a tree bad and its fruit will be bad, for a tree is recognised by its fruit. You brood of vipers, how can you who are evil say anything good? For out of the overflow of the heart the mouth speaks" (Matthew 12:33–34).

The tree represents the heart and the fruit of the tree what comes out of our mouths. The tree is known by its fruit. Therefore what comes out of our mouths is an indication of what is in our hearts. Jesus goes on to apply this very specifically to our words. "The good man brings good things out of the good stored up in him, and the evil man brings evil things out of the evil stored up in him" (Matthew 12:35).

James also argues this point: "Out of the same mouth come praise and cursing. My brothers, this should not be. Can both fresh water and salt water flow from the same spring? My brothers, can a fig tree bear olives, or a grapevine bear figs? Neither can a salt spring produce fresh water" (James 3:10–12).

Therefore we need to take note of Proverbs 4:23: "Above all else, guard your heart, for it is the wellspring of life." Or as someone once put it: "The mouth is the barometer of the heart."

We "keep our heart" by confessing our sins, being cleansed and forgiven. We need to come to grips with the fact that lying is a sin. Repentance is required for the cleansing of sin. It is a realisation and acknowledgement that our relationship with the Lord has been affected. The action of repentance involves a wilful decision to change the sinful action by the strength of God and the power of the Holy Spirit. "If we confess our sins to God he is faithful and just and will forgive us our sins and purify us from all unrighteousness" (1 John 1:9).

2. Refuse evil and yield to God

The second cure involves refusing evil and yielding to God. "Do not let sin reign in your mortal body so that you obey its evil desires. Do not offer the parts of your body to sin, as instruments of wickedness, but rather offer yourselves to God, as those who have been brought from death to life; and offer the parts of your body to him as instruments of righteousness. For sin shall not be your master" (Romans 6:12–14). We are to deny the devil access to the use of our bodies. Make a stand that the devil will not use your tongue and *yield yourself to God*.

Deliberately tell God that you want your heart and your tongue to be an instrument of righteousness and that you are yielding them to Him for that purpose. Pray as the Psalmist did:

> Create in me a pure heart, O God,
> and renew a steadfast spirit within me.
> (Psalm 51:10)

3. *Submit to discipline*

We need to be disciplined in the way we talk about one another. "If your brother sins against you, go and show him his fault, just between the two of you" (Matthew 18:15).

That is discipline. Do not go and tell everybody else first. That is our usual reaction. If somebody upsets me, I do not tell him – I tell everybody except the one who offended me, who will probably later hear through gossip! It is then harder to heal the breach.

Therefore, if somebody does something wrong (gossip, slander, lie, etc.), first go and speak directly to the person concerned. Secondly, and this is where most people slip up, if somebody comes to you and says, "Do you know what Harry said about me?", remember to ask, "Have you spoken to Harry?" If the reply is "No", then say, "Well, don't speak to me about it." That is real discipline.

Otherwise you can become responsible for making the situation worse and causing dissent in the body of Christ.

We must face the truth about our sinful lies and ask God to forgive us and cleanse us. Then we should accept His forgiveness, praying for the Holy Spirit to give us power and strength, love to help and heal people – and not hurt them – and self control. Make a positive decision to live out a life characterised by integrity and honesty. "What is hateful to you, do not do to your neighbour, that is the whole Torah, while the rest is commentary thereof" (Rabbi Hillel – The Talmud). And as Jesus Himself said, "For this reason I was born, and for this I came into the world, to testify to the truth. Everyone on the side of truth listens to me" (John 18:37).

10

> You shall not covet your neighbour's house.
> You shall not covet your neighbour's wife, or
> his manservant or maidservant, his ox or
> donkey, or anything that belongs to your
> neighbour.
>
> (Exodus 20:17)

The grass always seems greener on the other side of the fence. The conversation at the other end of the room is always more interesting than the conversation you are involved in. However long you take agonising over the menu deciding which sweet to have, when the person's next to you arrives, you realise you have made the wrong choice!

God made us a little lower than the angels, but most of us are concerned to climb a little higher than the Jones's. We see it even in the youngest of children – we want what we have not got.

It is interesting and significant that God chose this particular sin of thought. He could have chosen lustful thoughts – which most of us would think of as the worst sin of the mind and the sin that we are most conscious of. He could have chosen pride. But God chose the sin of covetousness. Covetousness is so often at the root of so much else and, in the end, it usually results in sinful words and actions.

To "covet" is actually a neutral experience. The Apostle Paul tells us we should covet prophecy (1 Corinthians

14:39) and covet the best gifts (1 Corinthians 12:31). We are free to covet good things. In being free to covet good things, we are of course equally free to covet the wrong things. This emphasises the fact that coveting wrongly is a deliberately sinful act.

Examples of covetous sins

The first covetous sin in the Bible is found in Genesis 3: "When the woman (Eve) saw that the fruit of the tree was good for food and pleasing to the eye, and also desirable for gaining wisdom, she took some and ate it. She also gave some to her husband, who was with her, and he ate it. Then the eyes of both of them were opened, and they realised that they were naked" (Genesis 3:6–7).

Eve saw the fruit and desired it. But God had said: "You must not eat fruit from the tree that is in the middle of the garden, and you must not touch it, or you will die" (Genesis 3:3).

Many other covetous sins are recorded in the pages of the Bible, including that of King David desiring Bathsheba. In time, David repented. His confession was not a cold, formal acknowledgement of guilt, but a true and heartfelt humbling of himself before God. It was a deep cry for pardon and for restoration to his heavenly Father's favour – as Psalms 32 and 51 clearly show.

In the New Testament, we are told about Judas Iscariot, a disciple of Jesus Christ who went to the Chief Priests and, in exchange for money, agreed to give them information regarding Jesus' whereabouts. Judas' desire for money even led him to betray Jesus. It's been said: "Still as of old, man by himself is priced. For 30 pieces Judas sold himself not Jesus Christ."

Judas not only sold himself, he lost himself. He excommunicated himself and went out to his own place (Acts 1:25) by hanging (Matthew 27:5). This story shows us that it is sadly possible to be associated with Jesus, to live with Him and hear His gracious words, to witness His wonderful works and yet refuse Him our heart's allegiance and so be lost.

Modern life is gripped by covetousness. Today the story is still the same. Richard Foster in his book *Freedom of Simplicity* writes: "Contemporary culture is plagued by the passion to possess." We are suffocated by a four-lettered obscenity – "more". But the irony about coveting is that the desire for more is not satisfied when we do get the possessions.

When Israel was given the tenth commandment, she was on her way to a land that God had promised. This land was flowing with milk and honey (Exodus 3:8,17). There was enough for everybody. Given this, you would have thought it quite unnecessary to include a commandment about coveting. God had promised that everyone would have enough.

The solution – materialism?

Many people agree that we are cluttered with possessions, that materialism is not the answer to the deepest cries of the human. Many believe this – but it seems to make very little difference in practice.

A journalist writing about people in Sweden expressed it succinctly: "Except for the climate, Sweden has everything. Money, education, peace, beauty, taste, full employment, welfare, weekend cottages, freedom, excellent food. These ought to combine to make the Swedes the happiest people in the world, but I found them to be discontented, restless with life, ridden with neurosis."

It is fine to know there is a problem – even to know that covetousness is the problem. But it still continues to grip us deep down inside and so we go on desiring and wanting more and more and more. To find the solution we need to understand how sin works. C. S. Lewis offers a very helpful picture of sin as a parasite: "The strength of a parasite depends on the strength of its host. The weaker the thing it is feeding on, the weaker it will be. The stronger the thing it is feeding on and the stronger the parasite can become." The strength of sin depends on the strength of the good thing on which it is feeding. Sin is not something that exists in isolation. It is a parasitic negative thing, a misuse of something good that God has created.

Covetousness – the positive aspects

Covetousness feeds on our good nature and on the healthy things in our life. The desire to be better people is a God-given desire. Having this motivation enables us to develop and grow, to improve and mature. These characteristics are good.

Back in Genesis, we are told that, "The Lord God took the man and put him in the Garden of Eden to work it and take care of it" (Genesis 2:15). Man was instructed to work and take care of the little bit of earth God gave him. The implication is that we should do the same. We have a God-given instinct to possess, care for and look after something – and not only a desire to care for possessions such as a garden or a home, but also a desire to care for people: "The Lord God said, 'It is not good for the man to be alone. I will make a helper suitable for him'" (Genesis 2:18).

We have a God-given desire to be responsible for other people – to feel for them, to care for them and to look after them. Caring for someone and something is good. To care for someone and something creates in us concern and consideration which are good characteristics.

Covetousness – the negative side

However, it is the strength of the good motivations and good qualities God has given us that makes covetousness so powerful. Sin works in us, against these good gifts. Sin takes the desire for progress ("to work [the garden] and care for it") and twists it into a selfish desire to be better than other people. In effect, the desire to care for things and people can become idolatrous. The moment we place greater value on created things than on the Creator, they become idols and effectively we worship them instead of God. "Put to death . . . evil desires and greed, which is idolatry" (Colossians 3:5).

It is the same story with people: people can become idols and the God-given desire to care for other people becomes a subtle desire to own and control them. We end up coveting them for our own good and they too become idols.

Covetousness is a distortion of the good characteristics and motives that God has given us. The Apostle Paul, like us, found that the more we are told that covetousness is wrong, the more the desire can be stirred up within us. "I would not have known what coveting really was if the law had not said, 'Do not covet'. But sin, seizing the opportunity afforded by the commandment, produced in me every kind of covetous desire" (Romans 7:7–8).

He goes on in the same chapter to explain that this does not mean that he did not covet before he was aware of the tenth commandment. He did, but the commandment actually made him aware of it. In fact, it made him so aware of it that it felt like it was gripping him more and more. True as the commandments are, they can leave us feeling frustrated, depressed and helpless. They are not meant to do that to us as Christians. God wants us to see what we ought to do so that we do not do what is wrong. In this case, He wants us to break out from the chains of covetousness.

Back to the beginning – our purpose, goals and ambitions

We need to see again that we live to bring God glory. Deep down, beneath all the covetousness we experience in our human nature, there is a longing for satisfaction. That desire is met and fulfilled in our relationship with God and experience of Him.

After thirty years of detours and dead-ends, Augustine – in his moment of surrender – found all that had previously eluded him and he wrote: "Our hearts were made for you, O God, and they shall not rest until they rest in you."

Covetousness, as we have said, springs from a good thing – ambition – in its best sense. Remember the Apostle Paul's goal and ambition: "I press on towards the goal to win the prize for which God has called me heavenwards in Christ Jesus" (Philippians 3:14).

Paul is gripped by a good, attainable ambition – to live to the glory of God and to fulfil God's plans and purposes. The more Paul is in line with what God wants him to be, the more he discovers his true self and the more he discovers genuine fulfilment. Our goal is to follow Jesus and to be more like Him. I heard a management consultant say: "A goal is more than a dream, it is a dream being acted upon, it is more than a hazy 'Oh, I wish I could.' A goal is a clear, 'This is what I am working towards.'"

There is a forest in France that is so big that people were constantly getting lost. So the authorities painted triangles on some trees. If you got lost, you found a tree and with your back to the triangle, you walked forwards and you would get out. To change the analogy, if we stand on the Bible – God's word – and fill our minds with the Word and fill our hearts with the Holy Spirit, we will discover insight and strength.

So what about possessions?

As for possessions, we need to see that they are a trust from God. This is the Bible's perspective on possessions: "All things come from thee, and of thy own have we given thee" (1 Chronicles 29:14, RSV). As well as getting enjoyment from our possessions, we have a responsibility for them. In our throw-away society, there is a danger of not taking care of possessions. Some Christians get a little neurotic about looking after things and so they make their shoes last longer and make their clothes last longer. This may seem to be Christian pettiness, but it is a good thing to look after the things that God has given us. To recognise that they have value and are not to be disposed of thoughtlessly is good. As with other things, we must not go over-the-top. We should be aware of and sensible with the changing society in which we live.

Being sensible about looking after things is right, but we must not let it become a subtle excuse not to share and not to strive for an equal, just society. Israel was given this commandment in a society that was geared to justice. There were carefully written rules in Old Testament economics – and there was a fair degree of equality in society. They were not petty rules. They were there in an attempt to avoid the possibility of one group becoming poorer and poorer – which is exactly what we see happening in our world today.

Most of us are confused and distressed when we come to
the subject of equality and wonder what we can actually do
about it in practice. It is a good start if we and our society
are continually aware of it. God does want justice in the
distribution of the good things of life. As Christians we
cannot accuse someone of being covetous who simply
desires enough food for him and his family to survive,
enough clothing and warmth, shelter and housing. It is
simply using God-given initiatives in God's world as He
meant us to. Nevertheless, poverty must not become an
excuse for covetousness. We can all consider ourselves
poor in relation to someone else. The moment we begin to
use our relative poverty as an excuse for covetousness,
we are falling back into sin. Both poor and rich can be
covetous.

G. K. Chesterton said: "There are two ways to get
enough; one is to continue to accumulate more and more.
The other is to desire less." Let us learn to be content.
Being positive about what we have rather than what we do
not have can have an amazing effect. Spurgeon wrote: "I
like going window shopping to see all the things I don't
need to buy." The Apostle Paul wrote: "I have learned to
be content whatever the circumstances. I know what it is to
be in need, and I know what it is to have plenty. I have
learned the secret of being content in any and every situation, whether well fed or hungry, whether living in plenty or
in want. I can do everything through him who gives me
strength" (Philippians 4:11–13).

Contentment is something that we need to learn and is
found in Jesus Christ. Again, Spurgeon said: "I looked at
Jesus and the Dove of Peace flew into my heart. I looked at
the Dove of Peace and she flew away."

There is a parable called "The Golden Windows" about
a little boy who lived in the Highlands of Scotland. The
little boy would look out of his bedroom window, across the

valley to a large house with golden windows. The boy thought the people living there must be superior to have golden windows and that he had better not ever go near that house. But curiosity would not leave him and one day he could not resist the urge to get close to the house with the golden windows. As he approached the house, he met another boy who asked what he wanted. He said, "I want to see your house with the golden windows." The other boy said, "That's ridiculous. What are you talking about? Where do you live anyway?" "I'm from over the valley." "Then you're the boy with the house with the golden windows." They turned and looked around. The sun had moved across the valley and was now shining in the windows of the other house.

It is so easy to covet what others have and forget that what *we* have is equally good, if not better. Of course, we may often wish we could own our own homes or car or have some little beautiful things around us. We have to face that and not let it turn us sour or destroy us. Let us be generous with however much we have, remembering the words the Lord Jesus Himself said: "It is more blessed to give than to receive" (Acts 20:35).

An old miser became a Christian and was beginning to work out the implications of his new-found faith when there was a knock on his door. It was a man from the village, whose house had burnt down, requesting some food for his family. The new Christian went to the kitchen to get him some meat and bread. On the way he kept hearing "give him a small piece of meat, only one loaf of bread – give him a small piece of meat, only one loaf of bread." He realised this was the devil telling him these things. As he stood deciding what to give, the devil said it to him again. The new Christian said, "Devil, if you don't shut up I'll give him the lot." As Paul wrote to Timothy, we should "be generous and willing to share" (1 Timothy 6:18). A fifteenth-century gravestone in England had these words inscribed:

> What we gave we have
> What we spent we had
> But what we kept we lost.

And what about people?

This applies not just to things but to people too. We need to grasp that God wants the best for other people. If we love a person we will want the best for that person. The best for them does not always mean they do what we want. It is of course hard to let go, whether they are our physical children or people we have learned to care for as teachers, because there is a great desire to go on possessing somebody's life. But we must let go, however hard and painful, and let God work in their lives. A deeper experience of love for other people will deal with coveting (a grasping of other people).

So let us enjoy what we have

Let us enjoy God's world: "the world of life or death or the present or the future – all are yours, and you are of Christ, and Christ is of God" (1 Corinthians 3:22–23). It is Christ's world and those of us who belong to Christ and are in Christ can enjoy it and appreciate it. We must not let covetousness destroy our enjoyment of God's world. If we see something and want to make it ours, then we feel bad if it does not belong to us. Consequently, it is destroyed as a beautiful experience.

Jim Elliott, a dedicated missionary to the Auca Indians,

kept a diary recorded in the book *Shadow of the Almighty*.

> I felt I must write something tonight in praise of the God of delight. All day the sun dropped hints of Spring and at dusk returning from the shops I exalted in the distant wall of purple in the hills, guarded by the unblinking venus. The night spread black and blossomed brilliantly with stars. It is exalting and delicious to stand with the mind tugging at your coat and the heavens hailing your heart, to gaze and to glory and to give oneself again to God. What more can a man ask? Oh the fullness, pleasure, sheer excitement of knowing God on earth.

We have seen that covetousness makes us want to be better than others. But God wants us to be ambitious – to be more like Himself and therefore more the person He wants us to be.

Covetousness makes us hungry for possessions, always wanting to grasp more. But God wants to give us enjoyment of the good things of life and set us free from the necessity to possess and grasp, touch and label things as our own.

Covetousness makes us want to possess people to build up our ego and to bolster up our own insecurities. But God wants to bring us into such a fulfilling, satisfying relationship with Him that we do not have to do that any longer. He wants to set us free to love people a little bit as He loves them. Jesus came to bring life in all its fullness (John 10:10).

LIFE MEANS WHAT?

J. John

What is life all about?

Is there anything beyond the here and now?

Happiness is elusive in the modern world. Fear, anxiety and loneliness are hallmarks of our society. Where is the cure? Wealth and possessions do not supply it, any more than fame, brilliance or good looks.

Where else can we look? To God?

NIV BIBLE

The New International Version is the most popular modern English Bible in Britain and the world.

Whether you need a Bible to carry around in your pocket, or one with notes and references to help you to study the meaning of the Bible in depth, you will find one to suit your requirements among the wide range of available editions.

"I have used the NIV for my own personal meditation for several years now, and feel totally at home with it."

Mary Pytches

"Having used the NIV Bible for personal study . . . I warmly commend it as an accurate, readable and sound translation of God's Word."

Rev. David Cohen
General Director, Scripture Union